Dedication

To my health visitor Kelly who
introduced me to Baby-Led Weaning
and to my children who were the perfect pupils

Acknowledgement

I would like to thank Angela Clarence for her editorial assistance
in preparing the manuscript for publication.

Baby-Led Weaning
Step by Step

Julie Clark BSc N.Med

Registered Nutritionist

Balloonview

DISCLAIMER:

This book has been written and published strictly for informational and educational purposes only. It is not intended to serve as a substitute for medical, dietary, healthcare or other professional advice. If you have concerns about any aspect of your child's health or development, you should seek advice from your health visitor, General Practitioner or other healthcare professional. Any use of the information in this book is made on the reader's good judgement and is the reader's sole responsibility.

Published by Balloon View Ltd, www.balloonview.com

Printed and bound in Great Britain by
CPI Group (UK) Ltd, Croydon, CR0 4YY

ISBN 978-1-907798-58-0

Chapters

Foreword

Introduction

1   What is Baby-Led Weaning?

Rosie's Diary – Have you thought about weaning?

2   Getting Prepared

Rosie's Diary – Two Weeks to Go

3   The Eating Begins - What is a Healthy Balanced Diet?

Rosie's Diary – Six Months Old and Ready to Begin

4   Month 6 - What to Expect

Rosie's Diary – Baby-Led Weaning

5   Month 7 - Reading Food Labels

Rosie's Diary – More Progress

6   Month 8 - The Nutrients Your Child Needs

Rosie's Diary – Already Eight Months Old

7   Month 9 - Using Supplements

Rosie's Diary – The Pincer Grip

8   Month 10 - Food allergies and intolerances

Rosie's Diary – Out and About

9   Month 11 - Getting Ready for their First Birthday

Rosie's Diary - Only two breastfeeds

10   One year old - What Happens Next?

Rosie's Diary - First Birthday

11   Picky and Fussy Eaters

12   My Top 10 Foods for Young Children

13   What the Parents Have to Say

14   Family Favourite Recipes

15   The Final Word

Foreword

"I would highly recommend baby-led weaning having weaned my own children using this method. As a GP I often see the result of poor diet and lifestyle, so seeing a baby develop a healthy relationship with food from the offset using the baby-led weaning method is something I feel should be promoted. The advantages I have experienced with my own children include relaxed family mealtimes and a real enjoyment of food. They also make very healthy food choices without me having to 'badger' them! Eating together is a real pleasure. I attended Julie's Happy Little Eaters course and found the information invaluable. I would recommend this excellent step-by-step guide to any parent or health care worker."

Doctor Hannah Warren

MBBS, BSc, MRCGP, DRCOG, DFSRH

"Julie's book is a welcome and invaluable guide for any parent or health care professional wanting to know exactly what Baby-Led Weaning entails, coupled with excellent nutritional advice for the whole family.

Baby-Led Weaning, is not a new concept. I have been recommending this method for a number of years and continue to be amazed at how skilled babies are at eating, making choices and regulating their appetites.

For many years, the guidance, unfortunately, was to wean early – and as babies were not developmentally ready to feed themselves, spoon feeding and purées were introduced. Following extensive research which showed that babies' nutritional needs were best met by an exclusive milk diet until 6 months of age (which coincides with most babies learning to sit, reach out and chew) the guidelines were changed in 2003."

Penny Lazell
RGN RHV Independent Health Visitor and Children's Sleep Consultant
www.healthvisitor4u.com

Introduction

I am a Nutritionist and a Mum and I have written this book to help you give your child the best possible dietary start in life by using the Baby-Led Weaning method.

Wouldn't it be great if your child could enjoy a family meal with you, sitting up at the table and eating the same foods as the rest of the family from the age of six months? This is exactly what my two children have done and there is no reason why you can't do it too.

Children who 'self-feed' tend to develop their motor skills more quickly, talk sooner and more clearly, are less likely to become fussy eaters and may have a reduced chance of becoming overweight or obese because they develop a good relationship with healthy food.

This manual has been written with all the nutritional and practical help for anyone who wants to practise Baby-Led Weaning but isn't quite sure how to go about it. It also incorporates a written and pictorial diary of my daughter Rosie as she discovers and masters self-feeding, in the hope that it will give you confidence to allow your baby the joy of feeding themselves.

Julie x

Chapter One

Before Starting Baby-Led Weaning

What exactly is Baby-Led Weaning?

Baby-Led Weaning allows your baby to feed themselves normal foods from the age of six months. This means that you will not need to spoon-feed or prepare puréed food because your baby will be able to pick food up and feed themselves. There are many advantages to allowing your baby to feed in this way, including a reduced risk of obesity, better social skills and improved motor skills but the most important advantage, I believe, is that they develop a much healthier relationship with food, which has a major impact on the future health of your child.

Is Baby-Led Weaning Right for You?

- Yes if you are prepared to cook from scratch
- Yes if you can tolerate a lot of mess
- Yes if your baby is developing at the right pace for their age
- Yes if you have discussed it with your health visitor and family

Your Concerns

The two most common concerns that parents have when feeding in this way are:

a. How will I know if they are getting enough food?
b. Will my baby choke?

You will find that during the first few weeks your baby will either spit out the majority of food you give them or simply play with their food. This is completely normal and is part of their learning experience. Some babies will start eating food almost straight away, whilst others can take up to three months (or sometimes longer) to get to grips with Baby-Led Weaning. Do not be concerned about the amount of food they are eating or not eating as your baby will make up the difference with their milk feeds.

Generally speaking your baby will be eating a balanced diet around the nine month mark. It is very common for a baby's weight to stagnate or drop a little when weaning this way. This can especially occur around the seven to eight month mark. This is because your baby will be trying to work out the correct balance between food and milk and this can take a little bit of time. Do not worry about this and do not feel pressured by anyone to give puréed foods unless there is a real reason for concern. Most babies will experience a growth spurt once they have really mastered Self-Feeding.

Once you get past these concerns and stick out the first few weeks, you will be surprised at how quickly and with what expertise a young baby can self-feed. All the parents who have been on my course rave about Baby-Led Weaning. You will almost certainly be pleased when you see the difference between your baby and a baby that has been purée-fed.

You can never completely eradicate the risk of choking and you should always take care when feeding young children. Baby-Led Weaning does not absolve your responsibility as a parent to supervise and monitor your child at feeding time. There is however, no increased risk using Baby-Led Weaning compared to a baby who has been fed purées and then moved on to finger foods. In fact there may be a reduced risk of choking because your baby will learn very quickly that food needs to be broken down before it moves to the back of their throat, otherwise they gag.

Gagging is a normal part of Baby-Led Weaning. When a baby gags it does not bother them, they make lots of noise and then continue to eat as normal. Choking on the other hand is silent as the airway is blocked and it is frightening for the child. When you first start Baby-Led Weaning your baby will have a sensitive gag reflex. You may have noticed that they sometimes gag when they put their hands in their mouths or when chewing on toys. This is a safety mechanism which prevents objects from going to the back of the throat before they are ready to be swallowed.

The gag reflex starts very far forward on a baby's tongue but as they get older this reflex starts to move back. This is an important and effective safety mechanism for self-feeding.

The first time your baby gags on food you will probably be scared and worried and want to get your child out of the highchair and help them. This is a normal reaction, although you must try to remain calm and allow your baby to deal with the food themselves. Some babies gag a lot for the first few weeks and even months and others only gag a couple of times when they first start feeding.

The best way for you to reduce the risk of choking is to firstly make sure your baby is sitting upright and not, in any way, leaning back and secondly, let them be solely in control of what food enters their mouth. Foods that present an obvious greater risk, such as whole grapes, can easily be cut in half. Never leave your child unattended with food.

If you are still concerned about choking, the best advice I can give is to attend a baby first aid course so that you are fully prepared for any eventuality. There is also some excellent guidance available on the NHS Choices website at www. nhs.uk. From the home page, type 'baby choking' into the search field at the top of the page.

Twins or More

If you are a parent of multiples, feeding time has the potential to be a massive challenge. However, I have had a number of parents with twins attend my courses and they would all urge you to let your multiples get on with it themselves. It will make your life easier, as well as giving them all the benefits that accompany this way of feeding.

Premature Babies

Generally speaking there is no reason why babies born prematurely cannot enjoy the benefits of Baby-Led Weaning. Unless there are concerns about their health or other factors involved, most premature babies seem to cope well with Baby-Led Weaning if they undergo it at the right age. You will need to be guided by their readiness, so read the section about signs for being ready to self-feed and I've found that their 'adjusted' age usually works well. So a baby born two months earlier will most likely be ready to self-feed when they are eight months old instead of the usual six months.

Do speak to your health visitor or consultant about this though and use your gut instinct as you will be the person who knows your child the best.

Now are you ready to get organised?

Key Points

- Read the first few chapters of this book so you know what is involved and how to get prepared.
- Talk to your family explaining the ins and outs of Baby-Led weaning and make sure everyone is in agreement.

Rosie's Diary – "Have you thought about weaning?"

The Health Visitor asks "have you thought about weaning?"

"No", I reply, "my baby is 6 weeks old, her poo is green, I have no idea what I'm doing and I'm struggling to breastfeed and recover from an emergency C-section."

Fast forward two months and I'm now ready to think about weaning. After all I am a nutritionist and food is very important to me. I'm thinking, like all parents, that I want my baby to have the best possible dietary start. I've heard the news and seen the evidence; our children are getting fatter and unhealthier. I start looking at the weaning kits and thinking about purées, I get a nagging uncomfortable feeling about it. I start asking myself "why can't my baby just eat normal foods?"

The Health Visitor asks "have you heard of baby-led weaning"? (I have not!) She tells me about not needing to purée food or spoon-feed the baby. My ears prick up!

The baby's asleep so I start researching baby-led weaning and BOOM, light bulb moment, cue the fanfare!

As soon as I started reading about Baby-Led Weaning, I realised that this way of feeding relates to my job as a nutritionist and the nagging, uncomfortable feeling I had when thinking about purées has gone.

My baby would eat and understand a healthy balanced diet, be in control of her appetite (just like breastfeeding) and would be included in our family meals, eating the same foods from six months old.

Common sense could and would prevail.

I now cannot wait to start the feeding journey.

Chapter Two

Getting Prepared

Ideally you should wait until your baby is six months old before you start Baby-Led Weaning as this is when their digestive system is ready to process solid foods. However, some babies will be ready around five-and-a-half months and others will not be interested in food until well after they turn six months.

If your baby was premature or has health issues, it is best to speak to your Health Visitor before choosing Baby-Led Weaning.

Babies usually need to start eating solids from six months, because this coincides with certain nutrient levels declining in breast milk. For example, iron levels start to drop after six months of breastfeeding and your baby will need to top up their iron stores with whole food. The nutrients don't suddenly disappear overnight, so don't be too concerned about this. Your baby doesn't need to start eating three square meals a day from six months to counter the decline in the vitamins and minerals from breast milk.

Solid feeding starts when your baby can show that he or she is ready for it. Usually it will begin by your baby trying to grab food from you, when they are able to sit up unsupported, when they can hold their heads up and when their milk feeds may not be keeping them satisfied.

A couple of weeks before your baby turns six months old, sit them up with you when you eat. Give them a cup and spoon to play with, as this gets them used to handling implements, as well as getting them familiar with their highchair.

When you sit your baby up to eat, you need to make sure that the tray is not too high for them or too far away. A Bumbo with a tray is a good option when starting out. With regards to highchairs, you want one that is easy to clean.

I personally use and recommend the Ikea plastic chair, which is an excellent size, easy to clean and extremely good value for money. Tripp Trapp also make a good chair.

Make sure your highchair is not ridiculously big for your baby. Check that they are well supported, can reach the tray and that the height is suitable. Imagine if you were trying to eat your dinner from a plate that was at your head height and too far away. Always consider things from your babies perspective. They are about to learn a new, difficult task so simple things, like being able to easily reach, are rather important.

Just one last point about highchairs, you do not need a reclining one. The highchair is used for the purpose of eating not sleeping!

You will need to buy some self-feeding weaning spoons (these are the shorter ones that usually say 'from 7 months' on them), a free flow beaker (one without a valve), some bibs (the ones with the arms are best) and something to go on the floor (a cheap table cloth or shower curtain from the pound shop are better than the rather small splash mats).

You won't need plates or bowls initially, as you'll tend to place food on their tray for the first few months.

Tell your family that you are going to wean your baby using the Baby-Led Weaning method and explain what this means. Get those around you ready for the weaning process. It can be very stressful if family members do not support your choice in weaning this way, so make sure you tell them the benefits and what can be expected during the initial few weeks. It is especially important that anyone looking after your child understands that your baby will be feeding themselves.

Your parents in particular may have concerns about this way of weaning because it will be completely alien to them. This can make you question your decision, especially when you see your parents react to a gagging episode! Trust your instincts and keep going because in a matter of a few weeks or months those who had the strongest objection will become the biggest advocates of this way of weaning.

Here is what my Mum and my Mother-in-Law had to say about Baby-Led Weaning.

"When the time came to wean my children, they were given soft foods like baby rice, rusk mashed in milk and puréed dinners - all fed to them, by me, on a spoon. So when my grandson's first solid food was introduced I was horrified to see a full roast dinner cut into pieces for him to pick up and put in his mouth. My first reaction was that he would choke on the pieces and also that if he couldn't swallow the food, he wouldn't be getting enough nutrients. I was soon to learn that these initial fears were unfounded as he didn't choke and appeared to be managing to feed himself well (even though a lot seemed to end up on the floor or spat into the bib)!

I now feel that Baby-Led Weaning is the way forward having watched both my grandchildren enjoying a whole variety of different foods whilst being 'a part' of family meal times. It has been an education for both the child and myself. Taking them to a restaurant, however, and letting them feed themselves was interesting to say the least - my granddaughter covered from head to foot in spaghetti bolognaise was something to behold!!!"

Sue (my Mum)

"When our children were ready to be weaned over 30 years ago, we were determined that they wouldn't be eating mass produced food in jars from the supermarket. They were given the same food that we ate, but blended to a texture that we felt appropriate. They were spoon-fed initially until they showed an interest in feeding themselves.

When our grandson, Charlie, was ready to be weaned, and Julie explained the "Baby-Led Weaning" concept, we were very apprehensive. How would such a small child cope with eating whole food? Surely it should be puréed! However, we watched in wonderment as he ate a Kiwi for the first time - separating the skin from the pulp in his mouth and then spitting the skin onto his plate. His first roast dinner was no problem at all. He enjoyed discovering all sorts of different foods and textures and yes he did gag occasionally, which alarmed me, but I soon learnt that this was quite a normal reaction. I noticed that allowing him to self-feed also helped him rapidly develop his hand to eye co-ordination and his speech.

We love that both Charlie and Rosie have been included in meals both at home and going out. I would highly recommend this way of weaning to anyone."

Lorraine (my Mother-in-Law)

It's time to get excited about starting the weaning process. Make sure your camera is at the ready!

Have a look at the foods listed below and the next time you go food shopping you can begin stocking up:

- Unsalted Rice Cakes
- Porridge (normal Scots porridge oats is fine)
- Oatibix, Weetabix or Shredded Wheat
- Nut butter (the brand Meridian do Cashew Nut, Almond and Hazelnut as well as seed butters)
- Sugar free jam (St Dalfour is a good make)
- Yoghurt with no added sugar (Plum, Ella's Kitchen or Rachel brands)
- Fruit that can be cut into strips (banana, mango, kiwi etc.)
- Vegetables (carrots, baby sweet corn, broccoli, peppers etc.)
- Cucumber
- Mild cheese
- Ingredients for homemade hummus (chickpeas, tahini, garlic, lemon, olive oil)

Key Points

- Go shopping and buy your highchair, beaker, spoons, bibs and mess control items.
- Get your baby used to sitting in their highchair or Bumbo a couple of weeks before you start feeding.
- Give them a spoon and beaker to play with and let them watch you prepare and eat your food.
- Make sure your diet is healthy NOW because when your baby starts feeding you should all be eating the same food together.
- Buy the suggested foods and let your baby see you try the food yourself before they start self-feeding as it will build their trust in the food.

Rosie's Diary – Two Weeks to Go

Rosie aged five months getting prepared! Will I be left or right handed.

Rosie is five-and-a-half months old. She is unable to sit up on her own but she can hold her head up really well. She is very interested in everything around her and is intently watching us when we eat.

She has been sitting in her Bumbo and experimenting with holding her spoon. We like to sit her in her Bumbo on our dining room table so that she can see what we are doing. She looks impatient to have a go herself, so roll on the 25th March when she will be exactly six months old.

Rosie is exclusively breastfed and is still waking up at night. She is a big baby but she takes her milk really well and goes four hours between each feed.

Two Days to Go

Rosie is more than ready for her first food. These past few days she has practically been launching herself at anything resembling food. Today she sat on my lap whilst I had some rice cakes with hummus and salad and she kept grabbing my arm to try and get at the food. I feel quite mean as she really wants to try some of the food we have. We are all getting excited about her starting on solids, particularly Daddy who would have caved in and given her something by now. Today she has been practising holding a Doidy cup (this is a tilted

Getting used to family meals!

baby-friendly cup) and has even managed to have a sip of water before tipping the remainder all down herself. She currently weighs 21lbs and is still waking up in the night for a feed. Hopefully this will change once she starts to get some food in her, as I'm exhausted!

Chapter Three

The Eating Begins

What is a healthy balanced diet?

Before you start weaning your baby it is important to understand what constitutes a healthy balanced diet and which foods a baby can and can't have, or manage, at this age. It is a good idea to look at what you are eating and make changes for the better before you start weaning your baby.

A balanced diet is made up of the following food groups; protein, fats, carbohydrates and fruit, salad and vegetables. The biggest mistake that people make when starting to wean this way is that they only feel comfortable giving their baby fruit, vegetables and bread. It is vital for growth and development that a baby eats from all of the food groups.

Your baby will learn how and what to eat by watching you and other members of the family. Setting a good example is the best way to ensure your baby eats a healthy balanced diet.

Protein

Foods containing protein include meat, fish, dairy produce, eggs, beans & pulses, soya, nuts and seeds. Proteins contain amino acids, nine of which can only be obtained from the food we eat. Amino acids are vital for proper growth. They also repair and maintain us and, when combined with carbohydrates, also provide energy.

Carbohydrates

Carbohydrates contain sugars that fuel every organ in our body. Glucose, the sugar obtained from carbohydrates, is essential for the proper functioning of your brain. Your body also needs carbohydrates for your bone, cartilage, tissues and nervous system. You also need this food group to provide you with energy. There are two types of carbohydrates, simple and complex. Simple carbohydrates are white and refined grains whereas complex carbohydrates are brown and wholegrain foods. Complex carbohydrates contain more nutrients and will release their sugars slowly into your body. This is much better for your health.

Foods containing carbohydrates include potatoes, rice, pasta, oats and bread.

Fats

Fats are essential. We need fat for energy, to protect our organs and to absorb certain nutrients (such as fat soluble vitamins). Fats also make essential hormones, build cell membranes and are vital for your brain. Your brain is made up of a lot of fat. Your immune system also relies on the anti-inflammatory role of essential fats. These fats also keep cholesterol levels under control and your blood less sticky.

Healthy fats (monounsaturated or polyunsaturated) are liquid at room temperature. Good fats improve your health. Unhealthy fats (saturated or trans/hydrogenated) are hard at room temperature and are found in processed foods and animal produce. Too much of these increase your risk of heart disease, strokes and cancer.

Good fats include olive oil, seed and nut oil, fish oil, rice bran oil, coconut oil, avocado oil and sunflower oil.

I prefer to use coconut oil, olive oil and rice bran oil for cooking as they have a very high smoke point making them safer to use. Fats can easily get damaged when heated, so those that have a high smoke point are more stable and better to use for cooking.

Fruits & Vegetables

Fruits, salads and vegetables provide essential nutrients including water, fibre, vitamins and minerals. They also contain phyto-nutrients and antioxidants which are key to staying healthy.

You will be aware of Government initiatives promoting 'five-a-day'. In other countries they have campaigns to encourage people to eat seven-a-day! The unfortunate fact is that a vast proportion of the British population fail to eat even five-a-day!

This food group is vital for ensuring good health. Numerous studies have shown that people who eat a high proportion of this food group are significantly less likely to develop the four major life threatening diseases (heart disease, stroke, cancer and diabetes).

Generally speaking a healthy plate should look something like this:-

How to Balance Your Food Groups

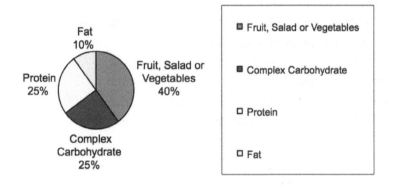

The exception with babies and young children is that they need a higher percentage of fat in their diet compared to an adult. Around 25-35% of a child's calorie intake should come from fat up until the age of two years. Your baby will get these additional fat calories from full-fat dairy foods and oils and fats from foods such as seeds and nuts (ground or in butter form until they are three years old).

What Can I give my Baby and What Foods should I Avoid?

At six months your baby will be able to pick up food in much the same way as they do their toys. They can only use their fist and do not have the ability to open their hand to get at the food inside. For this reason, their food needs to be either in a stick shape, big enough to stick out of their fist, or sticky enough to stay on a spoon.

The best first foods to try are:

- Fruits such as mango, kiwi, pear, banana or anything else soft (you can wash the skins and keep them on as this makes it easier for your baby to grip)
- Steamed or roasted vegetables such as baby sweet corn, broccoli, carrot, courgette, cauliflower, green beans, peppers, potato, sweet potato, butternut squash
- Sticks of cucumber and avocado
- Thin strips of meat
- Sticks of firm, mild cheese
- Unsalted brown rice cakes cut in to strips and topped with hummus or other dips/spreads
- Oatibix, Weetabix, Shredded wheat type cereals softened with a little milk
- Thick porridge loaded onto a spoon
- Mashed potato loaded onto a spoon
- Toast fingers, mini pitta bread
- Hard-boiled egg or omelette cut into strips
- The brand Plum do a thick Fromage Frais which is brilliant for loading on to a spoon

Salt

You need to be particularly careful with regard to how much salt your baby consumes, because their kidneys are still very immature. For this reason the recommended salt intake for your baby should be no more than 1g per day. This is an absolute maximum amount. The recommended maximum amount for adults is 6g - to put this in to context, a teaspoon of salt is equivalent to 3g.

Examples of the Salt Content in Food:

1 Medium Slice of Bread 0.45g
1 Rasher of Bacon 0.5g
2 Sticks of Cheese 0.3g
1 Teaspoon of Marmite 0.62g
1 Sausage 0.95g
1 Slice of Pizza 3.0g

Be careful when reading food labels as sometimes the salt is not given and sodium is listed instead. Sodium needs to be multiplied by 2.5 to get the salt figure.

Stock cubes and gravy granules are very high in salt. I use either Marigold Low Salt Vegetable Bullion powder or Kallo low salt stock cubes in my cooking. In my experience 'baby' stock cubes are tasteless and it's better to add herbs and spices to your recipes or make your own stock.

Foods to Avoid

1. Any processed or fast foods
2. Anything containing caffeine (this includes chocolate)
3. Whole nuts, fish with bones and fruit with stones (always cut grapes and cherry tomatoes etc. in half, due to choking hazard)
4. Salt (avoid ready-made foods as these will contain salt)
5. Sugar and artificial sweeteners
6. Honey (until they are one year old)
7. Fizzy drinks, squashes and undiluted fruit juice
8. E numbers, MSG, other flavour enhancers
9. Smoked foods (although a little smoked salmon is fine)
10. Foods in brine (such as tinned tuna or olives)
11. Soy sauce, ketchup and other ready-made sauces
12. Gravy made from granules or stock cubes
13. Very spicy foods

Foods to Limit

1. Hard cheeses - maximum twice a week (opt for mild rather than mature cheese)
2. Ham, bacon and sausages - maximum once a week
3. Baked beans - maximum twice a week
4. Most breakfast cereals (check the salt and sugar content)

Foods That May Be Tricky In the First Few Weeks

1. Apples (try soft pears instead)
2. Small orange segments like Satsumas (try large orange segments but check for pips)
3. Ryvita or other hard crackers (Rice Cakes with spread are better)

What Can My Baby Drink at Six Months Old?

At this age your baby should only be drinking breast milk or formula milk and water. Until they are twelve months old they cannot drink any other milk.

Always give your baby some water with their food in a valve-free beaker (tap water is fine).

Avoid the temptation to give juice or squashes as these will be high in sugar. I personally do not agree with the juice drinks available for young babies. Even pure fruit juice still provides a concentrated amount of sugar and just encourages a sweet tooth. Babies and young children do not need these drinks.

What do I do when my baby turns six months?

Decide on the exact day you are going to start weaning. Choose a day that isn't too busy so you can focus on this exciting milestone. When your baby wakes up give him or her the usual milk feed (it doesn't matter if this is formula or breast).

When YOU are ready to have YOUR breakfast, sit your baby up with you, either on your lap or in a Bumbo or high chair and give them two foods to try. Make sure you have mess control in place (bibs, floor mat etc). Put the food on their tray and let them decide what to do with it! You should also eat a little of what they are having, as well as whatever else you want for your breakfast. An ideal choice would be some banana and a toast finger. Give them a cup of water alongside any food. You do not need to boil water at this age. You can use water straight from the tap. You also do not need to sterilise their crockery and utensils at this stage, although if you want to, that's perfectly fine.

Use a Doidy cup (a baby friendly tilted cup) or a free flowing beaker. Do not use a valved beaker at this age.

Your baby will do some or one of the following:-

1. Ignore the fact that food has been put in front of them!
2. Pick up the food, squash it, look at it, stick it up their nose or in their eyes and then throw it on the floor or up the wall!
3. Pick it up, try it, pull all sorts of faces, and spit it out and then pick it up again!

At this stage the emphasis is on play. You do not need to be concerned about how much or how little they are actually eating. Remain calm and confident as your baby will pick up on your feelings, especially if they are having a gagging episode.

If your baby has eaten the banana and toast finger then give them some more. If they get irritable, take them away from the food and continue your day.

Carry on with your milk feeds as normal for the time being.

Because your baby is unable to use their tongue to dislodge food from the roof of their mouth or from the insides of their cheeks, make sure you check they have not squirreled any food away before you lay them down on their backs as this presents a choking hazard.

When lunch time comes, sit your baby up and give them some more foods to try. It helps if this is a version of what you are having. A rice cake with a little hummus, plus cucumber sticks, would be a good choice. If your baby is asleep at lunchtime then don't worry about them missing a meal. This will happen frequently in the first few weeks or months.

If your baby is hungry or tired do not overtax them by sitting them up to eat. This new skill will take a lot of effort and it can be very frustrating if they are tired and/or hungry. Treat all meal times as play. Keep their milk feeding schedule as usual.

When it comes to dinner time do exactly the same, sit them up with you and give them a version of what you are having. A good choice would be mashed potato with some fish and steamed vegetables. You can mix the fish with the mashed potato and load it onto the spoon for your baby. Just place the spoon either in their hand or on their tray.

Aiming a spoon toward their mouths will take a few attempts, as this is a difficult motor skill to learn. They may end up with food on their face before they get the aim right. This is all normal.

Keep portions small as they won't eat a great amount at this stage. Don't put too many items on their tray, as that can be overwhelming. Your baby's stomach is only the size of their two fists together. Keep some food in reserve in case they do decide to chomp it all down.

You will no doubt repeat this process for a couple of weeks. Each baby is different, so do go with your baby's specific needs. Some will want to play with their food and not eat a lot for two or three months, others will want to eat from day one!

Have your camera ready and enjoy the first few days.

What If My Baby is Starting Nursery?

You can still use Baby-Led Weaning if your child is going to be starting nursery. Remember that you are paying the nursery to look after your child how you want them to be looked after. Most nurseries are now fully aware of Baby-Led Weaning and although the majority will still prepare puréed foods, you can still ask that they only preload the spoon to let your baby be in control of feeding themselves.

If you have a Smartphone or a phone that takes video, then film your baby eating and show it to your child's key carer. That way they will have a good understanding of what your baby can do and how well they can feed themselves.

If it is logistically possible, do try to eat at least one meal a day with your baby, even if they are going into full-time child care. For example, have breakfast with your baby before taking them to nursery or have a light tea with them in the evening after you pick them up. Make the most of the weekends eating together and your baby will progress just as well.

Planning the First Week

To help you get organised and ready for when your baby turns 6 months old and is ready to start feeding, I have outlined a week's meal plan. This is simply a guide and you can use the suggestions or substitute your own, depending on the type of foods your family likes to eat.

Day	Breakfast	Lunch	Dinner
1	Banana cut into a stick shape. 1/3rd Weetabix biscuit softened with milk (preload on to a spoon and let your baby pick up the spoon).	Unsalted rice cake with cream cheese and cut in strips. Cucumber sticks and banana left over from breakfast	In a steamer place a small piece of salmon fillet, a small potato and vegetables such as carrot sticks, broccoli and baby sweet corn (you could also grill the salmon, roast the vegetables and boil the potatoes.

Day	Breakfast	Lunch	Dinner
2	Fromage Frais (use the Plum brand) pre-loaded on to a spoon - put the spoon in your baby's hand or let them pick up the spoon from the tray. Kiwi segment with the skin left on.	Jam sandwich using one slice of wholemeal bread with butter & sugar free jam. Fold the bread in half and cut into strips. Kiwi segments left over from breakfast.	Mashed sweet potato with steamed vegetables and grilled chicken breast cut in to a strip.
3	Porridge (use normal Scots oats) made thickly with water and milk, preload it onto a spoon for your baby to pick up. Pear, cored and cut into sticks, leave the skin on (if you prefer you can also grate the pear into the porridge).	Scrambled egg on wholemeal toast, add some milk to the egg to keep it soft and then you can press the egg on to the toast, cut into fingers. Tomato cut into wedges, use tomatoes big enough for your baby to hold.	Roasted vegetables (use onion, courgette, peppers, tomato) with homemade chips and a piece of grilled sausage. (Black Farmer Daughter Sausages are just the right size. You can also remove the sausage skin which makes it easier to eat.)
4	Wholemeal toast fingers with salt free butter and sugar free jam (use St Dalfour available in most supermarkets).	Unsalted rice cake with homemade hummus, cucumber and pepper sticks. Pear segments.	Shepherd's pie (adjust your recipe to reduce the salt).
5	Egg bread using wholemeal bread dipped in egg and fried in a little oil.	Cheese stick (use mild hard cheddar), cucumber and pepper sticks, tomato wedge.	Butternut squash curry with mashed potato (refer to recipe).
6	Choose any of the choices above that your baby enjoyed.	Choose any of the choices above that your baby enjoyed.	Lentil dhal with rice (refer to recipe).
7	Choose any of the choices above that your baby enjoyed.	Choose any of the choices above that your baby enjoyed.	Roast dinner - a strip of meat, roast potato segment, parsnip stick, carrot stick, broccoli spears (avoid gravy unless using meat juices).

Shopping List

- Banana
- Kiwi
- Pear
- Cucumber
- Tomatoes
- Lemon
- Peppers
- Potatoes
- Sweet potatoes

- Parsnip
- Carrots
- Broccoli
- Cauliflower
- Baby sweet corn
- Baby leaf spinach
- Onions (both red and white)
- Courgette
- Butternut squash
- Garlic
- Fresh ginger

- Organic full fat cow's milk (you can freeze milk into an ice cube tray and use as needed if the rest of the family are using skimmed or semi skimmed milk)
- Fromage Frais (the brand Plum with no added sugar) or natural yoghurt
- Salt free butter
- Eggs (organic preferably)
- Full fat plain cream cheese
- Salmon fillet
- Chicken breast
- Meat for roasting

- Weetabix
- Scots Porridge Oats
- Wholemeal bread
- Sugar free jam (the brand St Dalfour is available in most supermarkets)
- Unsalted rice cakes
- Extra virgin olive oil
- Tin of chickpeas
- Tinned chopped tomatoes
- Jar of tahini (this is ground sesame seeds)
- Paprika
- Red lentils
- Vegetable stock
- Tin of coconut milk
- Curry powder

Key Points

- Make sure you have your food cupboards stocked with Baby-Led Weaning ingredients.
- Decide on the day you are going to start and keep it as relaxed as possible as you and your baby will need extra time when you first start weaning.
- Keep your baby's milk feed schedule exactly the same for the time being.
- If your baby is tired or upset do not attempt to sit them up to eat and if they become irritable whilst eating take them away from the eating environment.
- Do not worry if you miss a number of meals in the first few weeks.
- Remember to lead by example and eat the same as your baby as they will learn by watching you.

Rosie's Diary – Six Months Old and Ready to Begin

The first day, for breakfast, we gave her some strips of mango with the skin on; a strawberry; a segment of kiwi with the skin on; a spoonful of porridge; and a spoonful of yoghurt. She tried everything managing very well with her spoon, but pulled all sorts of faces (it was as if we had given her the most disgusting thing in the world)! Shortly afterwards she seemed to react to the food. She rubbed her eyes a lot and they became swollen. This didn't seem to bother her too much. Our first thoughts were that it might be the yoghurt, since her older brother is dairy intolerant, but after giving her the foods again over the next few days we discovered that it was the strawberry that had caused the problem. The swollen eyes lasted a few hours and by the following morning she was perfectly fine.

The first week has been all over the place; sometimes she was really interested and other times she would ignore the food. We made a dinner of lemon sole, sweet potatoes and sautéed spinach mashed all together and loaded on to the spoon for her - she ate four spoonfuls and really enjoyed it.

Other foods we thought she would really like didn't interest her that much. The foods she likes the best are orange segments, yoghurt and broccoli.

The mess is something else! She likes to sit in her Bumbo and enjoys drinking the water from the Doidy cup or the Tommee Tippee Free Flow Beaker. Sometimes she shudders when she tries the food. I loaded up a spoonful of porridge for her and she managed to catapult the entire spoonful all over the kitchen – very funny!

This week she has fallen asleep around lunchtime so she has missed lunch quite a lot. She has continued with her milk feeds as usual, having one in the morning around 8am, then at 11.30am and 3.30pm and then a couple of times before bedtime at 7pm. Her sleep patterns are very erratic; sometimes she sleeps from 7pm until around 5.45am; other nights she wakes a couple of times.

As a breastfed baby she would often go a day or two without a bowel movement. Since weaning she has definitely gone more often. A couple of nappies have been brown instead of the usual yellow. We have also noticed that she is able to sit up on her own now; something she couldn't do two weeks ago!

Rosie demonstrating in her first week of Self-Feeding that she can pick up a rice cake, a spoon and a piece of mango (both at the same time!) and direct these to her mouth, plus manage an open topped cup whilst having fun!

What We Had To Eat This Week:

Breakfast – Oatibix with a little soya milk/rice milk or cow's milk; scrambled egg on brown toast; strips of mango/kiwi with the skin on; Plum Fromage Frais; porridge made with mostly water and a little milk; toast fingers with cashew nut butter.

Lunch – Unsalted rice cakes with homemade hummus; steamed carrot and baby sweet corn; cherry tomatoes halved; grapes halved; orange segments; sugar-free jam with cashew nut butter sandwiches on brown bread; chicken strips; cucumber sticks; and celery sticks.

Dinner – Oven cooked lemon sole with sautéed spinach and new potatoes; sausage, homemade chips and steamed vegetables; chicken stir-fry made with 5 spice, chilli, ginger and garlic; roast chicken with steamed vegetables and roast potatoes (no gravy); omelette with new potatoes and salad.

Chapter Four

6 Months Old, What to Expect

During the first month of Baby-Led Weaning you will feel as if you are always preparing food, thinking about food, clearing up food and eating food as well as watching the clock to fit in milk feeds and naps. If you are also breastfeeding you can feel a little overwhelmed when you first start out. This is normal and I promise you it will not always be this demanding.

You may have a baby like Rosie who takes to eating almost immediately or you may have a baby who shows little interest in eating and just wants to play and then cry when they have had enough. Every baby is different and you just have to trust your instincts and give this way of weaning a bit of time.

It can be frustrating when you go to a lot of effort to make food from scratch only to find that it ends up not eaten or on the floor.

To make life easier always try to give your baby a version of what you are having, that way you will only be preparing food for yourself plus a little extra for your baby. The main adjustment to make to your cooking is to avoid salt as much as possible.

You can cook and use normal milk with food but until your baby turns 12 months old they should not be given milk to drink. Until your baby reaches their first birthday they should only be given water and breast milk or formula to drink.

You do not need to use any special baby products such as baby rice or porridge.

The main emphasis at this stage is to have fun and enjoy mealtimes together. Tell your baby the names of the food you are giving them and what the colours are, as this is a great learning opportunity. If possible, let them see you preparing the food.

Try not to get too excited when they pick up food and put it into their mouths. You want the entire event to be normal. I'm sure no one praises you when you eat your dinner. Try not to stare at your baby! You will probably have to tell the Grandparents not to stare either!

The main thing to remember at this stage is that your baby can only pick food up in their fist, so food needs to be stick shaped. Also that they need to be able to reach their food, so check the position of the high chair if using one. It will be tiring for them when they first start out, so do not attempt to sit them up if they are hungry or tired and be sure to continue with your milk feeds as before.

Milk Choices

You can use milk in your cooking as soon as your baby is 6 months old but they cannot use milk as a drink substitute for breast or formula milk until they are 12 months old because it does not give them the correct amount of nutrients.

We tend to think of milk as only coming from a cow but these days there are a number of options which you may like to consider. And if your baby is dairy intolerant or you want to keep dairy intake low due to health concerns, the table below can help you decipher the varieties on the market.

	ADVANTAGES	DISADVANTAGES	HOW TO USE
Goats Milk	The protein in goat's milk is easier to digest and can occasionally be used by babies intolerant to cow's milk. Good source of calcium, protein, fat & vitamin A. Goats are not over-farmed as much as cows.	Goat's milk still contains lactose so is not suitable for lactose intolerant babies. It contains less B12 than cow's milk.	Can be used in exactly the same way as cow's milk. Nanny Care produce an excellent powdered product. Legislation allows goat's milk in infant feeding formulas.
Soya Milk	A good source of calcium, protein and phyto-oestrogens. Low in sugar. Gives a good creamy consistency which is nice in porridge.	Dairy intolerant babies often have problems digesting soya milk and soya products. Intake should be limited to avoid hormone disruption in girls particularly due to phyto-oestrogens.	Can be used in the same way as cow's milk but it will curdle if used in tea or hot drinks! Make sure you choose brands that are from non-genetically modified sources.

	ADVANTAGES	DISADVANTAGES	HOW TO USE
Almond Milk	A good source of vitamin E and is usually fortified with calcium and vitamin D.	Low in protein, fat and calories. This is ok if you are trying to lose weight but not great for a baby or young child. Can contain a number of additives.	Always choose the unsweetened variety and check for any artificial sweeteners. Better used cold, with cereal for example. Easy to make yourself.
Rice Milk	The least likely to cause allergy issues. It has a nice, sweet taste and is great for cooking.	Low in protein and fat but high in carbohydrates and sugars. Contains inorganic arsenic so intake must be limited.	Works well when making a white sauce.
Oat Milk	Good source of fibre, calcium (if fortified), vitamin E and folic acid.	Contains gluten so not suitable for anyone intolerant. Low in protein.	Can be used in the same way as cow's milk.
Coconut Milk	Contains vitamin E, B and C, as well as minerals magnesium and potassium. Also a rich source of lauric acid which is found in breast milk.	Low in protein, calories and calcium.	Best used in cooking including curries and soups. Check ingredients and make sure to buy the purest version available.
Hemp Milk	Very easy to digest. Good source of essential fats and protein plus many other vitamins and minerals.	Low in calcium (but usually fortified, check the brand).	Can be used in the same way as cow's milk.

Calcium is abundant in nearly all foods and our ability to absorb calcium from milk products is substantially less than from green vegetables. Whilst we do need to have the right levels of calcium to stay healthy, it is extremely easy to do this on an entirely dairy free diet. Milk has only been touted as the best source of calcium since the early 1900's. Unless your child is dairy intolerant I would recommend using goat's milk from one year old.

My preferred choice of milk for those on a dairy free diet is a mixture of oat and hemp milk, although it is useful to use some of the other milks from time to time as they all have different levels of nutrients with corresponding health benefits.

The plant, seed and nut based milks are very easy to make yourself. It simply involves soaking the product in filtered water and then straining through a muslin bag. For more information on the exact process have a look online.

Key Points

- The first month should be about play, learning and fun. Do not expect your baby to eat very much at this stage.
- Always check your baby's mouth before laying them on their backs just in case they have saved some food for later.
- Keep mealtimes as normal and relaxed as possible, do not stare at your baby.
- Name the foods you are giving your baby and describe the colour, texture and even where the food comes from, as they are absorbing a great deal at this age.
- Stay calm and enjoy this fantastic new stage.

Rosie's Diary – Baby-Led Weaning

Week 2

This week Rosie has been sleepy in the mornings so has missed breakfast a few times. And she has either been eating everything or hasn't bothered to eat solids at all. When she doesn't want her food, she removes it all from the tray and drops it over the side! If I load up a spoon and hand it to her, she holds it to the side and then lets it go. But she really enjoys sitting in her Bumbo, so we haven't had to worry about her getting stressed during a meal as she sits quite happily until we have all finished.

She has missed a few lunches due to napping, but some days has eaten well at all three meals. On the days when she has eaten a lot, she has definitely reduced her milk feeds. On average she is having 3-4 feeds during the day, followed by a feed at bedtime and then one feed during the night. She has gone through the night on one occasion this week.

Her hand to eye coordination is really coming along and after only two weeks she can easily direct the spoon from the tray to her mouth. She has also been able to pick up smaller food from her tray (quicker than her elder brother I think). I expect she will get her pincer grip very quickly.

Her nappies have been very interesting this week; she has had a number consisting of very full brown stools with some undigested foods present!

At just week two of self-feeding, Rosie is perfectly happy sitting in her Bumbo and showing her hand to mouth co-ordination whilst tucking into roast potatoes, carrots, green beans and roast chicken.

What We Had To Eat This Week:

Breakfast – much the same as last week but we also had a cooked breakfast with poached egg, bacon, grilled tomato and mushroom.

Lunch – much the same as last week but also included some sticks of mild hard cheddar cheese and feta cheese.

Dinner – homemade fish pie, pasta twirls with vegetables and tuna in a tomato sauce, roast chicken, vegetables and roast potatoes, plus some of the same as the previous week.

Week 3

This week has been quite challenging! Rosie has been getting on exceptionally well with her food and has really taken to most things she's been given. She seems to enjoy melon and pear in particular as well as kiwi, broccoli, carrot and yoghurt. However, Rosie may be teething as she has been very erratic with her sleeping and feeding, has bright red cheeks and lots of dribble.

She has also been suffering very badly with constipation and her bottom is very red. This is the first week that she has been really swallowing the food but despite the constipation she continues to eat well. She has been straining, going bright red in the face and then on occasions has screamed when she has passed a very small stool. She has been having a bath with Epsom salts morning and evening for the last two days, as well as homeopathic treatment and reflexology, so hopefully the constipation will pass as it is not at all pleasant.

Her hand to eye coordination is extremely precise and she is getting very good at picking up small foods. She likes pear and is determined to pick up any left-over bits almost using a pincer grip. It will not be long before she does get her pincer grip.

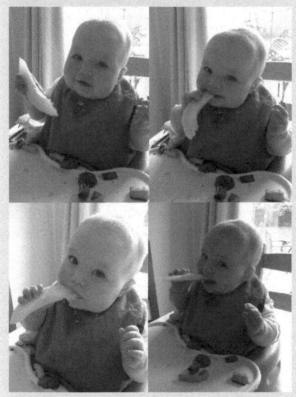

She loves her Tommy Tipee Beaker and drinks quite a lot of water. She is still using the Bumbo, but we have also purchased the Ikea highchair. Baby-led weaning is messy, so the easier a high chair is to clean the better!

Rosie is still not sleeping through the night, so last night I did not give her a feed when she woke up. I changed her nappy and then put her back in her cot with her lullaby music and lights on. She cried for about 15 minutes and then went back off to sleep from 4am until 8.30am; a clear indication

Rosie is really enjoying her melon and is able to hold the skin side so it doesn't slip out of her fist.

that she is not hungry, as her last feed was 11pm!!! But generally she is having three to four breastfeeds, plus one at bedtime and then one during the night. There is no pattern to her naps and quite often she doesn't sleep during the day.

This week she has been waking up at around 8am and then having her breakfast with her older brother and myself. Once I've got her cleaned up and changed she has been having her breastfeed. She doesn't seem to mind this at all. She then tends to have a feed late morning and then we have lunch. She has another feed around 3-4pm and then dinner is about 5-5.30pm. She goes to bed at 7pm and has a feed just before. She then wakes up at some point in the night and I will usually give her a feed, although last night she had a feed at 11.30pm and then woke again at 4am when I just changed her and put her back down.

This week she was also weighed to check her progress. At the start of her weaning she was 21lbs and this week she weighed 23lbs. It is very common for babies to drop a little weight or flatline when starting out with Baby-Led Weaning, so an increase of 2lbs is very good.

What We Had To Eat This Week:

Breakfast – lots of fruit, natural yoghurt, Oatibix, porridge, French toast, Kallo Puffed Rice and toast with cashew nut butter and sugar free jam.

Lunch – rice cakes with hummus or nut butter, cherry tomatoes, cucumber, cheese sticks, roast chicken strips, soft boiled egg and fruit.

Dinner – homemade fish pie (a definite favourite), sausage with roasted vegetables and new potatoes, salmon with mashed and steamed vegetables, pasta twirls with vegetables and tuna in a tomato sauce, roast chicken, vegetables and roast potatoes plus some of the same as the previous week.

Week 4

Our suspicions from last week were right and Rosie now has two bottom teeth. Teething can really upset the Baby-Led Weaning process, sometimes causing a disinterest in food. Before the teeth arrive the gums and mouth can be very sore and trying to eat solid food can be painful. Sometimes a baby will prefer to take puréed food as they can suck it to the back of their throat without having to break the food down with their tender gums. If you think your baby may be teething and they are losing interest in the food you are giving them, you can always use mashed or puréed foods loaded on to the spoon for them to feed themselves. Do not be tempted to opt for spoon-feeding as you will disrupt the progress you have made with Baby-Led Weaning.

This week Rosie had her first outing to a restaurant. We took a small packed lunch for her and she thoroughly enjoyed the bread dipped in olive oil and balsamic vinegar and had great fun picking up olives with tooth picks! One of the biggest problems eating out with a baby this young, is that most of the high chairs used in restaurants are the wooden type without a tray. The high chair itself is fine, but without a tray, or proper access to the table top, most of the food ends up on the floor! It can be frustrating when you have a limited food supply with you but your baby will soon get better at handling food - so don't let it put you off eating out.

Rosie is still suffering from constipation this week, but in the last couple of days (and ironically since her teeth have appeared) she has been passing a more normal stool. She is still waking up at night and there is no pattern as to what time, so when we go to bed we never know if she is going to wake up two hours later or seven hours later. It's frustrating, but is a normal part of demand feeding!

Today Rosie has eaten a huge amount of food. She swallowed the majority of the food for the first time, including chicken strips. Her favourite food this week (it does change) includes broccoli, yoghurt, sweet potato and cherry tomatoes. Last week she really enjoyed kiwi, but this week she has pretty much ignored it.

Rosie eating out for the first time at a restaurant. Most of the food ended up on the floor because these types of highchairs do not have a tray and your baby will tend to scoop the food from the table and it will end up falling through the gap!

Some babies will avoid foods to which they are allergic, almost ignoring that they exist on the tray. This is exactly what Rosie has been doing with egg. It's been served as an omelette, poached, hard boiled, scrambled and soft boiled and yet she is refusing to even touch it!

Her breastfeeds continue as the previous week with three to four feeds during the day plus one at bedtime and one in the night.

What We Had To Eat This Week:

Breakfast – *strips of kiwi, melon, orange segments, pineapple, pear (lots of fruit) plus Oatibix, porridge and toast.*

Lunch – *rice cakes with hummus, cheese spread or nut butter, cherry tomatoes, cucumber, cheese sticks, roast chicken strips, ham and fruit.*

Dinner – *same as the previous week, but this week we had jacket sweet potato, stir-fry chicken and chickpea curry.*

Chapter Five

7 Months Old

The first few weeks of Baby-Led Weaning are mainly about play and getting in to a routine. You get used to the constant need to be thinking about food, making food, eating food or clearing it up! Your baby will be getting used to picking up food, playing with food and hopefully eating some.

You will probably notice that most of the food they actually manage to get into their mouths falls back out again, because at this stage they haven't quite worked out how to chew and swallow. You will get so used to finding their food on the floor, in their bib or down the side of their high chair that the first time they actually eat something you won't quite believe it!

Something else to be aware of in the early stages is that whilst we, as adults, can use our tongue to dislodge food or clear our mouths, your baby cannot yet do this. Sometimes food will get stuck to the roof of their mouth or between their gums and cheek. Before you lay your baby down after mealtimes always check to make sure nothing is lurking inside.

Learning how to use the tongue and facial muscles is exactly how your baby learns to speak. Teaching so many babies to wean this way I have observed that one of the benefits of Baby-Led Weaning is advanced speech development. It makes sense when you see how quickly they build up their tongue and facial muscles dealing with the food they are eating.

Whilst many babies start teething around this age, some won't have teeth until they are nearly 12 months or even older. However, this doesn't stop them from being able to chew and swallow food. If you've ever put your finger in a baby's mouth and have them gum down on it, you'll know how strong they are. My oldest, Charlie, ate an apple when he was 9 months old with no teeth.

From the outset it is important to include good protein sources such as strips of meat. Although babies at this stage are unable to chew the meat, they can suck out the nutrients and discard the rest - their way of accessing the nutrients they need.

Usually around the end of this month your baby will start to open and close their fist, which means that they can start to get at the food inside that fist. This is a great development as they will start to pick up fistfuls of food and push it directly into their mouths and will often use the other hand to stop it all falling back out.

However, they still need food presented in a chip or stick shape, or food that can adhere to a preloaded spoon.

Sugar

Your brain relies on the sugars it gets from your carbohydrates and fruits to keep it running and your body has some rather complex and important ways to ensure you eat enough to keep your brain functioning. But the substance we call sugar has no nutritional value whatsoever even though it tastes nice and once we get a taste for sugar it is very hard to turn back.

Have you ever gone food shopping when you are hungry and then looked in your trolley to find it full of naughty treats? When your blood sugar drops, your body makes you seek out sugar in its most easily absorbable state; biscuits, cakes, chocolates and sweets.

Before the availability of sweets and confectionery and before the advent of industrialised processed foods in the 1960's, we would have obtained the sugars we needed from a whole-food diet. The sugar came from natural foods like fruit.

Your baby is still prehistoric in the making and is therefore completely able to obtain the sugar he or she needs from natural foods. The longer you can keep a sweet tooth at bay, the better it will be for your child. You will no doubt be aware of the increase in Type 2 Diabetes and obesity, which are all linked to the consumption of too many calories from sugary foods.

It is therefore important to keep your baby's diet low in refined sugars. Foods that tend to be high in refined sugar are obviously sweets, cakes and biscuits, but there are some that may surprise you. Breakfast cereals, pasta sauces, condiments and yoghurts can all have extremely high levels of sugar.

In particular, check the labels on yoghurts next time you go shopping. Yoghurts aimed at children and babies from four months can have as much as three teaspoons of sugar per pot. Breakfast cereals can have around 20-40% sugar, so again, please check the labels.

To give you an idea, most food labels will have the nutrients listed per 100g. You can use this as a visual percentage guide. So an item containing 32g of sugar per 100g has 32% (1/3rd) sugar. That is a lot!

Try to avoid any foods that have more than 10g of sugar per 100g (or 10%).

Foods that are advertised as low fat will tend to be high sugar and those advertised as low calorie will usually be high in fat.

1 teaspoon of sugar is equivalent to 5g. Always check the size of the serving so that you can calculate the amount of sugar and/or salt in a product.

Here is a comparison between a natural food and a processed food:-

Foods (per 100g)	Typical Serving	Calories	Carbs	Sugar	Fat	Saturated Fat	Salt
Porridge	50g	359	60.4g	1.5g	8.1g	1.6g	trace
Kellogg's Frosties	50g	375	87g	37g	0.6g	0.1g	0.9g

Note the calories are almost the same but where are the calories coming from? The Frosties contain 37g of sugar compared to the porridge at only 1.5g. It is quite easy to be on a low calorie diet that is high in sugar and low in essential nutrients!

When reading labels, the only exception to the sugar rule is if the product contains a lot of fruit. Always check the ingredients to see where the sugar is coming from. If the ingredients list sugar, glucose, syrups (or anything ending in 'ose') then the product should be avoided. If the sugar is coming from dried fruit then it is okay in moderation. A product that lists sugar within the first three ingredients should be avoided.

Generally speaking cooking from scratch and giving your baby natural whole food is best until they are at least 12 months old.

How much food should my baby be eating?

When you wean this way you are giving the control of how much food your baby consumes to them. Your baby is the only person who knows how much they want or need and when they are full.

Weaning this way is slower not only because your baby must learn to negotiate the food from tray to mouth, but because your baby is beginning to digest food in the correct way. Digestion starts with the sight and smell of food, followed by the action of the enzymes in saliva during the chewing process, and then completing in the stomach where the automatic 'feeling full' signals are sent to the brain. You may have been told many times that eating slowly and chewing your food properly can aid weight loss because it takes your stomach 20 minutes to tell your brain it is full. This has significant advantages when looking at appetite control. It may also be why babies weaned this way tend to have a reduced chance of becoming obese later in life. When food is puréed they don't get a chance to explore the sight and smell, or to chew, so the whole process is short circuited.

It is important to trust your baby when they eat lots of food one day and not much another. They may eat plenty from one food group at one time and loads from a different group at another time. This is completely normal but always have extra food in reserve, in case they are having a hungry day.

If your baby is upset or unwell they are very likely to refuse food or show little interest. A simple cold can really affect a baby's appetite and it can take some time to get back to normal. If your baby is also teething, their gums will be sore and they will not feel much like eating because it will be too painful for them.

Your baby will now start to adjust the amount of milk feeds taken, based on how much food they are consuming. This comes more naturally to breastfed babies as they are used to feeding on demand and have already started to understand their appetite. With formula fed babies you may need to adjust the milk feed for them. You can do this by reducing the amount per feed or you can try cutting out one of the bottles and see what happens.

Once you start weaning you will need to use the correct formula for this stage.

So if your baby is on a hungry formula this should be adjusted to the follow-on formula.

Some babies are so used to getting their calories and nutrients from their formula milk that they take a little longer to get in to self-feeding. This is nothing to worry about as long as they are happy and content. If you are at all concerned you can speak to your Health Visitor.

Below is a general guide to portion size:-
A serving is the size of your child's hand in a fist or their palm. You can also use this for yourself and older children. Make sure you go by what your child wants though; the fist/palm is just a general guide.

Protein – as a minimum, your child needs at least one portion (one fist) of animal sourced protein a day or two portions of vegetable sourced protein a day as a minimum. Ideally aim for protein at all meals but especially lunch and dinner. This includes meat, fish, eggs, beans, pulses, nuts, seeds, dairy and soya.

Carbohydrates – your child needs a portion at each meal, that's one fistful of carbohydrate at breakfast, lunch and dinner. This includes potatoes, crackers, bread, rice, oats and pasta.

Fat – your child needs more fat than an adult until they are three years old. It is therefore recommended that full fat products be used until they are three. After this you can opt for semi-skimmed versions in order to keep saturated fats (such as butter, cream, animal fat etc.) within safe limits. However, it is not advisable to switch to low fat until they are five, when your child's need for the additional fat is reduced (unless of course this has been advised by a medical professional). Breast milk is 50% fat and formula around 40%. These fats are made up of the essential fats (found in fish, seeds and nuts) as well as some saturated fat.

Fruit, Vegetables & Salad – your child needs two portions with each meal, that's two fistfuls of a different variety of fruit, salad and vegetables.

Remember to be guided by your baby as they are all different. A baby that is given control to self-feed will not usually overeat or starve themselves!

How Will I Know if my Baby Has Had Enough Food?

If you as an adult have eaten a large meal and have overindulged then you will probably place your knife and fork on your plate and push your plate away.

Your baby will do much the same. When they have had enough to eat, the majority of babies would rather not remain sitting in their high chairs looking at the remains of their food! Your baby will tend to let you know they have had enough in one of three typical ways.

1. They will cry and want to get out of their high chair as soon as possible.
2. They will use their arm to sweep the food from their tray.
3. They will individually pick up each piece of food and either hand it to you or drop it over the side.

If you get any other responses please let me know!

What about Milk Feeds?

If you are using formula milk then you should be using the follow-on stage (number 3). This makes allowance for the fact that your baby will also be getting calories and nutrients from food. If you have been using hungry baby formula you should no longer need this. You do need your baby to be hungry and want to eat the food you are giving them! If they are getting everything they need from the formula milk then they may show little interest in trying any solid food. If you are at all concerned about your baby's milk feeds, then please discuss this with your Health Visitor explaining that you are doing Baby-Led Weaning.

For breastfed babies you can simply continue as you have been, as your baby will let you know when they want to drop any feeds. As your baby starts to take in solid food you will probably notice that they automatically reduce the time they breastfeed.

Key Points

- Continue to remain relaxed at mealtimes and let your child continue to play with their food, developing at their own pace.
- Don't worry if they don't seem to be taking food down, they will when they are ready.
- Check your portion size, your baby's stomach is only the size of their two fists together.
- Make sure you are keeping sugar to an absolute minimum; particularly check the labels on breakfast cereals and yoghurts.

Rosie's Diary – More Progress

7 Months Old

Wow! Rosie is already 7 months old and is doing really well with feeding herself. The two teeth she now has are being put to good use and she is really getting stuck into foods like chicken. This weekend she featured at a Baby & Pregnancy Event, demonstrating Baby-Led Weaning. She showed her ability in picking up and eating broccoli, cauliflower, baby sweet corn, feta cheese, cherry tomatoes and sandwich fingers followed by melon wedges and orange segments. Good job she was hungry! She also decided it would be really good to show everyone the gag reflex, the little monkey!

A couple of weeks ago my husband sorted out breakfast for Rosie so I could have a lie in. How wonderful you may be thinking! Well yes, except for what he fed her! He knows the guidelines - making food from scratch, without salt or sugar, but he ended up feeding her honey on toast! Honey should not be given to children under one year old because of the botulism risk. After my initial panic I reminded myself that botulism is in fact rare and I just kept an eye on Rosie over the next few days to make sure nothing happened. I would like to remind all Baby-Led Weaning Mums that men also need to read the step by step guide!

We have moved Rosie from the Bumbo to the Ikea chair. She is extremely happy in this high chair and I am very pleased with how easy it is to clean. She is now swallowing food at breakfast, lunch and dinner and rarely misses a meal. I've even given her an afternoon snack on a number of occasions. She likes Organix flavoured rice cakes which I keep in my bag when we are out and about.

Last week we had tiger prawns in a tomato sauce which Rosie really enjoyed, eating four of them which is extremely impressive! Another recent favourite is lentil and squash curry which she has now had twice and on both occasions has managed to eat a small bowlful.

Rosie showing off her skills at the Baby and Pregnancy event; enjoying kiwi fruit; and lots more foods at home.

I am continually shocked at the amount of added sugar in baby yoghurts and Fromage Frais. We have been using Rachel's First Yoghurt which does not contain any added sugar. Rosie really likes it and can easily eat half a pot (the pots are full size which I find a bit odd for a baby yoghurt!).

This week I've also been looking at breakfast cereals. We generally use Oatibix, Shredded Wheat or porridge as these are all wholegrain with little or no added sugar. The majority of breakfast cereals contain high levels of sugar and salt. Take for example Apricot Wheats; these contain 20% sugar!

Rosie's milk feeds have now reduced. On average she has four feeds in the day and one during the night. She is showing signs of dropping the night feed and has slept through from 6.30pm until 7am on a number of occasions (although not enough for my liking!). I think she will also drop the late morning feed soon as she is eating so well at breakfast and lunch.

We are off to Spain next week so I will look forward to reporting Rosie's Baby-Led Weaning progress from the sunshine!

Chapter Six

8 Months Old

By this month things should have started to calm down. You will have got yourself into a routine of cooking, eating and clearing up and it will no longer feel like your entire day is spent dealing with food. Your baby will also be getting into a routine and you will probably find there is less waste to deal with.

You will have noticed by now that when your baby does manage to eat something it will show in their nappy fairly quickly. In the early days, food will often come out in almost the same way it went in. It is usual to see undigested and recognisable foods in your baby's stool. Colours will also be varied and will reflect the type of foods eaten. Watch out for beetroot as this can make a nappy look very red and frighten the life out of you! You must remember that your baby's digestive system is brand new and it will take a while to get used to the different foods that go in, are processed and emerge the other side.

By this age most of your babies will be eating and enjoying at least some, if not all of their foods. There will be some babies that take a little while longer, so try to be patient as the process can suddenly just click and then they are off with no looking back!

The majority of babies will be starting to use their fingers rather than their palms to pick up the food. The pincer grip (the use of the forefinger and thumb) will almost be there which enables them to pick up smaller items and a wider variety of food. They can tackle halved cherry tomatoes, Satsuma segments and even clumps of rice. Give them a go with a spoon and fork to try scooping up or stabbing their food.

You will have gained confidence by now and any gagging will just be part of the normal routine. However, it is really important that you are calm and confident at feeding times as your baby will pick up on your feelings. Try to make sure that anyone else present is also positive and confident.

Include your baby in as many family meals times as possible, especially at the weekend as babies learn so much by watching and interacting with everyone else. Eating together increases a child's sense of belonging as well as developing their trust in food (because you are all eating the same thing), which encourages them to try new foods without any issues; they will also be learning social skills such as etiquette and manners. Families who eat together also tend to plan, troubleshoot and solve problems together and have a better relationship with each other. Once you get into the habit of having family meals together, you will be reinforcing traditions and memories. There are some studies that show children obtain higher academic grades if the family eats together.

What Nutrients Does My Baby Need to Get from Food?

Vitamins

Vitamins are naturally occurring chemicals essential to health. Most of these come from food. with the exception of vitamin K and Biotin, which are made in your gut, and vitamin D, which is made in the skin with the help of sunlight.

Vitamins are essential for normal growth and development. They are used for many chemical reactions within the body, helping the body to use the calories in food, process fat, protein and carbohydrates and are involved in the repair and building of cells and tissues. They are crucially used as anti-oxidants to neutralise free radicals. Free radicals are the result of normal functions that are undertaken in the body. Think of it as the ash that is left after burning a fire. The antioxidants help clear up the debris left by free radicals. If left 'uncleansed' these free radicals cause damage in the body resulting in disease.

A good variety of foods and particularly colours are important to ensure a good intake of vitamins.

Cooking and processing methods can destroy vitamins, so try to eat fresh produce in season as much as possible. Using a steamer for cooking helps retain nutrients but if you do boil your vegetables, always keep the water and use it for stock. Many vitamins are water soluble so when you cook vegetables in water the vitamins dissolve into the cooking water and invariably get poured down the sink.

Phytochemicals

These are naturally occurring protective chemicals found in plant food. Evidence has shown that people who eat a diet high in phytochemicals i.e. those who consume plenty of fruits and vegetables, have a lower incidence of cardiovascular disease, diabetes and some cancers.

Antioxidants

All fruits and vegetables contain high levels of antioxidants and different colours have different levels and types of antioxidants. Antioxidants are needed to counter free radicals and other dangerous toxins in our bodies. They keep us from premature ageing and protect our cells from damage.

Minerals

Minerals are substances that occur in rock and metal ore. They are essential for health and are only needed in tiny amounts.

A good variety of different foods are important to ensure a good intake of minerals. Processing methods destroy the mineral content of many foods.

Why Your Child Needs Certain Nutrients

Energy - vitamins B & C, iron, magnesium, iodine and chromium

Bones - calcium, magnesium, vitamins D & K and boron

Growth & Repair - zinc, B-vitamins and folic acid

Immunity – vitamin C, antioxidants, selenium, zinc and essential fatty acids

Brain – essential fatty acids, B-vitamins, zinc, iron and selenium

Eye Health – vitamin A, carotenoids and vitamin C

Lung Health – carotenoids, antioxidants

Heart Health – magnesium, essential fatty acids, vitamin E

What Does RDA Mean?

RDA stands for Recommended Daily Allowance and is set by the Government. It is the minimum daily dose of each nutrient needed to avoid becoming ill – for instance, you need 60mg of vitamin C to prevent scurvy. The RDA is NOT the amount needed for optimum health.

Food with Good Sources of Vitamins:

Vitamin A
Sweet potato, carrots, cabbage, kale, spinach, butternut squash, peppers, apricots, orange-flesh melon, mango, liver and eggs.

Vitamin B1
Peas, spinach, whole grains, nuts, soya beans, meat.

Vitamin B2
Asparagus, cottage cheese, yoghurt, meat, fish, eggs.

Niacin
Peas, meat, fish, beans.

Pantothenic Acid B5
Sweet potato, avocado, mushrooms, meat, fish and beans.

Vitamin B6
Potato, sweet potato, bananas, poultry, fish.

Vitamin B12
Dairy produce, eggs, beef, seafood.

Biotin
Cauliflower, mushrooms, egg, fish, beans.

Folate
Sweetcorn, asparagus, green vegetables, beans.

Vitamin C
Fruits and vegetables.

Vitamin D
The sun is the main source, but small amounts can also be found in fish and eggs.

Vitamin E
Nuts, seeds, soya beans, wheat germ.

Calcium
Spinach, almonds, tofu, yoghurt, cheese and milk.

Magnesium
Whole grains, beans and pulses, nuts and seeds.

Iron
Spinach, dried fruit, red meat, eggs, pulses and beans, fish.

Selenium
Brown rice, Brazil nuts, fish, whole grains.

Zinc
Seafood & fish, nuts & seeds, meat, whole grains, beans.

Chromium
Fruit & vegetables, whole grains, eggs.

Essential Fatty Acids (Omega 3, 6 & 9)
- Omega 3 – salmon, mackerel, herring, tuna, sardines, flaxseeds, pumpkin seeds, walnuts
- Omega 6 – sunflower seeds, sesame seeds, pumpkin seeds, safflower oil, evening primrose oil, corn oil, soya oil
- Omega 9 – olive oil, almonds, walnuts

A Note on Wheat

Wheat is the most common cereal consumed in the UK. Wheat flour is used first and foremost for making bread. Other products that use wheat include cakes, biscuits, crackers, pastry, pasta and breakfast cereals. It is also used in the manufacture of beer and other alcoholic drinks and is a major source of feed for livestock. Wheat starch and gluten are major ingredients used in the food industry.

As a Nutritionist I tend to see a lot of people including young children who are intolerant of wheat, or more specifically the gluten inside the wheat grain.

Gluten is a protein that is extremely hard to digest. It makes digestion slow, difficult and incomplete due to its sticky consistency and molecular structure. For this reason I advise that you limit your baby's intake of wheat-based products to once a day and if possible go one or two days a week with none at all. For example if you have given your baby Weetabix for breakfast, use rice cakes for lunch and have potatoes at dinner. If you are planning a sandwich at lunchtime then have an oat-based breakfast and rice for dinner. Don't forget that bread has a good deal of added salt, so keeping to this rule will help keep your baby's salt intake under control.

Be aware that wheat is also found in soy sauce, Oxo-type stock, some crisps and sweets.

Dropping Milk Feeds

As I mentioned earlier, when you first start Baby-Led Weaning you will be keeping to the same milk feeds that you had been giving leading up to the six month start point. This will be the same whether you are breastfeeding or bottle feeding.

Even if you are breastfeeding you will most likely have a routine to feeding and even set times of the day when your baby is hungry.

The first few weeks of weaning your baby will mostly be playing with their food and they will be unlikely to be eating too much. It is therefore important that you continue your milk feeds exactly the same as you did before commencing weaning.

Once your baby starts swallowing and digesting some of the food, you can look at dropping a milk feed. If you are breastfeeding you will probably notice your baby reducing the time they feed or even showing little interest in one of their daytime feeds. This is perfectly normal. You have given complete control to your baby and they will tend to adjust how much milk they take in, depending on how much food they are eating.

With bottle feeding you may need to adjust the feeds yourself as your baby will be used to taking a certain quantity at certain times of the day. For example, you may want to try dropping the mid-morning feed so that your baby can eat a little more at lunch time. You will need to be guided by your baby as they are all individual. If your baby is showing little interest in food they may just be full up on milk. Always make sure you use the correct stage formula for your baby.

If you are unsure about what to do with your baby's milk feed then do speak to your Health Visitor for advice and explain that you are Baby-Led Weaning.

Key Points

- Make sure you are including your baby in as many family meals as possible as this will really help their progress.
- Check you are giving your baby plenty of variety so they have a range of different nutrients.
- Keep wheat products (i.e. bread, flour and pasta) to a maximum, once a day only as they are very hard to digest.

Rosie's Diary – Already 8 Months Old!

Off to Spain to visit Nanny and Granddad for a whole month. An early start means that we breakfasted at the airport in Costa Coffee with Rosie's meal of Kallo Puffed Rice with Soya Milk and a big helping of fruit popped in to our 'Klip it & Go' range of Tupperware dishes. These are particularly useful for keeping liquids and solids apart until you need to mix them.

I had made up a picnic of rice cakes and cashew nut butter, cherry tomatoes and chopped fruit for the flight. With Rosie on my lap, eating was a little messy but we managed to clean up afterwards. As Rosie is still being breastfed, I fed her both on take-off and landing as it is helpful for preventing the build-up of pressure in the ears. You can do the same with a bottle-

Rosie and her brother in the Spanish sunshine.

fed baby, as it's the sucking motion that helps keep their ears clear - the baby alternative to yawning or pinching your nose and blowing. Flying can be a painful experience for them otherwise, particularly during take-off and landing.

Once in Spain, Rosie really took to her new chair. Nanny had bought the kind that clips onto the table and the small gap between the chair and the table meant that a lot of the food ended up on the floor! We soon got wise to this and put a tray underneath to catch everything. Nanny is a great cook and Rosie's particular favourites are Shepherd's Pie and Chicken Risotto.

Rosie is the star attraction at the beach. I don't think Baby-Led Weaning is the norm yet in Spain, so seeing such a young baby eat so many big chunks of food was of particular interest. That, and the fact that she loved mixing sand into her picnic! We certainly did seem to attract a lot of attention.

Spanish tapas are proving to be a real hit with Rosie, so when eating out she is mostly able to share my food. The breadsticks that are always provided here are also a favourite, although I can't allow her to eat many due to the salt content.

We are into a good daily routine with Rosie taking a late morning nap in her pushchair and then having a long afternoon sleep in her cot. She is still waking during the night and having a feed. However, during this final week she has been sleeping through the night. I am still giving her a feed early morning and then again late morning, then late afternoon and at bedtime. However, she doesn't seem bothered if she misses some of these feeds.

In true Baby-Led Weaning style, Rosie tries to grab anything that I'm eating, especially if she doesn't have food of her own to hand. One day at the beach I'd been eating an ice-cream and Rosie practically launched herself at it. Since she was so determined I let her have some, although this is not something I would encourage!

There has definitely been an increase in the quantity of food that Rosie is now eating and there is a lot less wastage. She is doing well with picking up *her food and can open her fist and get at the food inside. She is so close to getting her pincer grip. Babies usually seem to 'get it' around the nine month mark and I think Rosie will be spot on with that milestone.*

During our month in Spain Rosie has grown significantly. I cannot report her weight as I haven't visited a weigh-in clinic but she has grown out of a lot of 6-9 month clothes, so I guess the sunshine and Nanny's cooking have had an effect.

I also wanted to include in my diary this lovely email I received while I was in Spain from a previous member of my Baby-Led Weaning course.

"I thought I would share with you our success with Baby-Led Weaning. Harrison is now nine months one week and four days old. We have been practising Baby-Led Weaning since he was six months old when we started very ad hoc with a few bits of what we were eating here and there. After a few weeks we started doing breakfast every day and then moved onto lunch. We didn't do tea until maybe six weeks down the line. Now Harrison has three square meals. In the last two weeks we have introduced snacks and offer him milk in his beaker at 11am and 3pm. He almost always chooses to eat the food rather than have milk and seems very contented with this option. He has a milk feed in the morning of about 6 oz although he can have more if he wants it, and has a bedtime milk feed of 7 oz. He still has a night feed of 6 oz but I am hoping this will stop soon.

He eats soooo much food it is a joy to see. He investigates everything and tries everything he is given. He loves pancakes for breakfast. Tuna croquettes and cheese straws have been a huge hit. Plums are by far his favourite fruit and he loves natural yoghurt with them.

I wanted to thank you so much for the information from your course. It was a real eye-opener to eating healthily and making sure Harrison has a healthy relationship with food. I don't have to lift a finger when I feed him, I get to eat a hot meal and I get to enjoy it.

We are well along the road of weaning and he is doing great!

Thanks again."

Chapter Seven

9 Months Old

This is the month where it all just seems to click. I have seen a number of Mums who are struggling with Baby-Led Weaning and getting frustrated and concerned that their baby is not eating anything or eating very little after 8-10 weeks of weaning. If this is true for you, please try not to worry, as your baby is about to 'get it'. Of course if you are seriously worried or if their weight has dropped considerably, then speak to your Health Visitor to get some advice. However, it is not uncommon for a baby's weight to stagnate or even drop when weaning this way, but when the self-feeding really clicks, they often undergo a massive growth spurt.

Your baby most probably has developed their pincer grip and is now able to pick up the smallest of foods and use both hands to make sure they keep the food in their mouths. Try giving them some raisins and/or peas to see if they can pick them up. Once your baby has achieved a good pincer grip they can really manage almost any food. Beans and pulses will not need to be mashed and if your baby is anything like my children, they will thoroughly enjoy actually picking out and eating any beans present in their meals. Beans and pulses are great to include in your baby's diet, as they are extremely high in nutrients and fibre and are low in fat. Add beans like cannellini (white beans) to pasta dishes or stews, add kidney beans to pasta dishes or Shepherd's Pie and use chickpeas wherever possible.

Soup will present a challenge at this stage because lifting a spoon and keeping it level is a very difficult skill to master so try putting soup in a cup for your baby to pick up and drink. With runny foods in general, put something alongside that can soak up the juice; bread or rice cakes with soup; and mashed potato with stews. You can try using bowls or plates but be careful, as most nine month old babies still enjoy throwing tableware about!

Your baby may be on the move. Crawling or shuffling will increase their need for food, so you can add a snack in the afternoon if you find they need it. If they have dropped the afternoon milk feed, they will very likely appreciate a snack of fruit, or a couple of flavoured rice cakes. Some babies may even be walking at this stage, although this is fairly unusual.

Should I be giving my Baby a Vitamin Supplement?

The NHS recommends that breastfed babies be given vitamin A, C & D in the form of drops from the age of 6 months while formula fed babies already have these vitamins added to the milk powder. Do ask your Health Visitor for more information about this.

As a nutritionist, I recommend that babies be given vitamin D drops if they are breastfed. I am not as concerned about vitamins A & C because the majority of Baby-Led Weaning babies will be eating lots of food that contain these nutrients such as mango, sweet potato, butternut squash, kiwi and oranges to name but a few. Vitamin D on the other hand is different as it relies on our exposure to the sun. In recent years there has been a great deal of research into the effects of vitamin D deficiency and the evidence is so conclusive that I give all of my family a vitamin D supplement and recommend that you do the same. I personally use Biocare's Vitamin D drops for Children and Nutrigold's Oral Spray for Adults.

Key Points

- Check your baby's pincer grip by giving them some peas or raisins to pick up.
- If you are breastfeeding, speak to your Health Visitor about a vitamin D supplement.
- Add some beans and pulses to your cooking as these are nutrient dense and are a great source of protein for growth and development.
- Your baby may experience a growth spurt at this stage as they really get to grips with self-feeding.

Rosie's Diary – The Pincer Grip

9 Months Old

Rosie has been true to form and at nine months old has really 'sussed out' how to eat and has achieved her pincer grip. It is so exciting to see her using her thumb and forefinger. Rosie is clearly enjoying this new skill and she likes to carefully pick out the peas and eat them before tackling the remainder of her dinner!

Rosie also has six teeth. So together with her pincer grip anything goes. She can really eat a wide variety of foods. Baby-Led Weaning babies usually only put into their mouths what they can safely pick up and chew or gum. Many babies at this stage will only just be getting their first teeth, but they naturally tend to select foods they can manage to break down and swallow. If your baby can pick up a raisin or pea, then you know that they can handle these small foods without a great risk of choking.

As well as achieving the pincer grip, Rosie has also mastered sleeping through the night. Hurray! At nearly ten months she has taken considerably longer than her older brother, who slept through from 13 weeks. I completely and totally commiserate with anyone whose baby is not sleeping through. Coping with sleep deprivation is hard and I have really struggled over the last couple of months. Rosie still wakes up occasionally, but six out of seven days a week she will sleep from 7pm until 7am. However she seems to know intuitively the days when I've got to be up early for work, as these are the nights she chooses to wake me up at 4am, the cheeky monkey (or similar words not to be spoken here!!).

While we are still breastfeeding, Rosie has dropped her feeds to three times a day. Generally speaking she has a feed around 11am, another at 3pm and then one just before bedtime at 6.30pm. It's difficult to know exactly what quantity of milk she is getting as she feeds so quickly (two minutes maximum on each side). If you are bottle feeding you will probably be giving three feeds of 210ml or 7fl oz. although every baby is different, especially if you are demand breastfeeding. I recently tried to express some milk but couldn't get anything to come out so I am assuming that my milk supply has reduced to match Rosie's needs.

For breakfast Rosie is eating porridge, Oatibix, mini shredded wheat, puffed rice or toast with unsalted butter and sugar-free jam. She always has a selection of fruit and about once a week I give her eggs, although she is not really that keen, unlike her brother who would have 'eggy peggy' every day!

For lunch the old favourite, Kallo Unsalted Rice Cakes, are usually on offer with either hummus, nut butter, cheese, ham, chicken or tuna, plus cherry tomatoes, grated carrot, strips of pepper and cucumber. Sometimes I make her a sandwich (using only one slice of bread due to the salt content – 0.5g per slice of bread is common) with any of the above fillings. Since getting her pincer grip, Rosie also quite enjoys a mixed bean salad. I will always give her some fruit or yoghurt afterwards. She absolutely LOVES yoghurt. We use either plain natural yoghurt, Plum Fromage Frais or Rachel's My First Yoghurts, as they don't have added sugar.

In the afternoon, Rosie usually has a snack of a few flavoured rice cakes, or Organix biscuits or fruit.

Dinner is now extremely varied. Rosie is very capable of eating almost

Raisins, Sweetcorn, Orange Segments and Pesto Rice!

anything, although foods that are runny still remain too challenging. She prefers to have her dinner tipped onto her tray and will often choose to use her hand rather than a loaded spoon. She seems to have a taste for curry and mildly spicy foods with rice. She is happy to eat roast chicken dinner, vegetarian chilli, lentil and squash curry, lasagne, pasta in general, lamb tagine, chicken curry, salmon fillet and fajitas. We always have steamed vegetables and her favourite is definitely broccoli.

If your baby has reached this stage, give them some corn on the cob, which is really good fun for them to eat. If they have their front teeth, give them half an apple to bite on. As you can see from my photographs, Rosie thoroughly enjoys her corn on the cob!

Chapter Eight

10 Months Old

After just four months practising Baby-Led Weaning with your baby, not only will you be amazed at their progress, but also at how easily you have incorporated healthy meals in to your family's daily life.

Your baby is probably eating so well by this stage that you will need to keep a close eye on unnecessary treats! When grandparents and other doting relatives see your child eating so competently you will find that sweets and chocolates materialise as if by magic!

The longer that you can keep these foods away from your child, the better. At ten months your baby doesn't even know what a 'treat' is. We have a massive obesity and diabetes problem in this country and in the whole of the Western world. The main reason for this is not too much fat, but too much sugar. Sugar is added to practically all processed food and low-fat products are notoriously high in sugar. Even food that we think of as healthy, including breakfast cereals, cereal bars, yoghurts and even bread, contains so much added refined sugar that it is not hard to see where we are going wrong.

When too much sugar floods your body, it has to go to work to rectify the problem. High levels of sugar circulating in your blood are not good for you. Your pancreas sends out insulin to bring your blood sugar down and this complicated process results in sugar being stored as fat! So when you keep flooding your body with sugar, your pancreas has to work incredibly hard and can start to struggle. This can cause insufficient quantities of insulin being secreted or cause insulin resistance, because the cells are so tired of having to take up the excess sugar. This results in conditions such as pre-diabetes, diabetes, hypoglycaemia and syndrome X.

Unfortunately our brain depends on sugar to function properly, so even a slight dip in your blood sugar levels can have you reaching for something sweet. The key is to give your body foods that do not contain refined sugars, but foods that release sugar slowly and which keep both your brain and your body happy.

You may recall the food group diagram in chapter 3, where sugar, unsurprisingly, does not feature. The sugar source should be coming from natural foods such as fruit and complex carbohydrates like oats.

Making sure your baby is only getting sugar from good food sources goes a long way to ensuring that they will live a long and healthy life. The longer you can avoid 'treats' the better.

We have a rule in our house - until you can ask for it you can't have it!!

After four months of getting to grips with the cooking and preparation of food to suit all the family, you have probably got a standard repertoire of recipes. Now would be a good time to make sure you are not stuck in a rut! Check to see if foods high in salt, or ready-made foods and snacks are not creeping in too much. Remember that even though your baby is more than capable of eating an entire cheese sandwich on their own, they still cannot handle more than 1g of salt a day. A cheese sandwich made with two slices of bread will take them over that allowance, so just be careful.

Are there any foods that you haven't tried to give your baby yet? Olives, Fennel, Scallops, Oatcakes?

Pomegranate seeds are a good one to try when your baby has a fully developed and refined pincer grip. Foods like spaghetti bolognaise are also good fun and you may want to try liquid type foods in a bowl.

In fact, if you find that your relatives want to treat your little one, then a great gift at this stage would be a Hungry Caterpillar or Gruffalo dinner set, or something along those lines, so that you can progress from putting food on their tray, to dishing up meals on a plate or in a bowl.

How Can I Tell if My Baby Has an Allergy or Intolerance to Food?

When your baby first starts on solid food, they can have some minor reactions as their bodies adjust. The most common one is redness around the hands and face, especially when trying foods like tomatoes. This is very normal and you shouldn't worry.

When a baby eats something that disagrees with them, they often let you know about it by screaming and getting very upset. A rash may have appeared which could be very uncomfortable, so a shower or bath will help. A rash around the trunk that occurs after eating, on a regular basis, can indicate intolerance to something. Babies tend not to touch the foods they know disagree with them. You may have already noticed their tendency to avoid certain foods, but it is helpful to keep an eye out for this.

The most common foods that cause allergy and/or intolerance are as follows:

Cow's milk, Wheat, Gluten, Yeast, Egg, Cashew nuts, Garlic, Soya, Brazil nuts, Almonds, Corn, Hazelnuts, Oats, Lentils, Kiwi fruit, Chilli, Sesame seeds, Sunflower seeds, and Peanuts.

Food allergy is different from food intolerance in that it is a rapid response by the body's immune system to a particular food. In this type of reaction, the body's immune system mistakes a food for an 'invader', often resulting in a rapid allergic reaction - within minutes. This type of allergic reaction is commonly associated with nuts and seafood and needs urgent action as it can be life threatening. It is however, rare, occurring in approximately 5% of the population (mostly children) and can be genetic.

Known as IgE, the skin, gut and airways are the usual areas for this type of reaction to manifest. Symptoms include, but are not limited to: rashes, stomach cramps, vomiting, coughing, wheezing, sneezing, and in extreme cases swelling of the lips, throat and face. These symptoms need to be treated and diagnosed by your GP and a Nutritionist can help you plan your diet to avoid the allergy trigger.

Another type of food allergy or intolerance is a delayed onset allergy, known as IgG, and this is much more common, affecting as many as one in three people. This type of reaction is complex, making it difficult to diagnose and treat. It often involves three or more foods, whereas the IgE reaction usually involves no more than two foods. Diagnosis is usually via an elimination diet and food/symptom diary.

Symptoms classified by Allergy UK include the following:-

Abdominal pains	Syndrome	Fluid retention	Sinusitis
Aches and pains	Diarrhoea	Headaches	Skin problems
Asthma	Eczema	Lethargy	Stomach cramps
Arthritis	Fatigue	M.E.	Tension
Bloating	Fibromyalgia	Restless Leg	Urticaria
Constipation	Irritable Bowel	Syndrome	Weight loss
Chronic Fatigue	Syndrome (IBS)	Rhinitis	Wheezing

In children, diseases and illness linked with allergies include ADHD, autism, asthma, eczema, bed wetting and recurrent ear, nose and throat (ENT) infections.

Typical symptoms to look out for in young children and babies include reflux, persistent coughs, constant runny nose, loose stools, skin problems and recurrent ear, nose and throat problems.

If you suspect an allergy (IgE), you need to see your GP as soon as possible but if a reaction has occurred that involves swelling, then go to your nearest A&E.

If you suspect intolerance (IgG), first write a food diary for a week and see which foods you are using the most. You can try to eliminate these for a short time to see if symptoms improve. I am experienced in treating this type of allergy and it is not easy to solve on your own. It is advisable to seek professional help when eliminating foods, especially where children are involved. I use muscle testing (Kinesiology) to test for allergies as well as private blood tests. Always see your GP first to rule out any other underlying problems.

Key Points

- If you have been putting food on your baby's tray up until now, try them with a plate instead. Be ready in case they hurl it at you!
- Make sure you are not stuck in a rut with your food choices and try something different.
- Do not allow 'treats' such as sweets and chocolate, your baby is still only 10 months old!

Rosie's Diary – Out and About

10 Months Old

This month we had a number of outings including the Happy Little Eaters annual Baby-Led Weaning picnic. This is a yearly event for all those who have attended my course. It's always great to get everyone together as some of the children are now four years old and some babies have only just started on their Baby-Led Weaning journey.

Brother and sister enjoying tagliatelle and Rosie on a picnic

We all went to the local pub for a meal out. It was interesting to see how Rosie ate the pub food neatly from her bowl, while her three year old brother was making the biggest mess ever. The only downside to Baby-Led Weaning I've discovered is that some children prefer to use their hands rather than implements for quite some time!!!

Up until now I have put Rosie's food on her tray a little at a time. Recently I've tried giving her a whole bowl or plate of food. Most of the time this works well, but there are many occasions when the bowl or plate is turned upside down or thrown onto the floor. She thinks it's a great game as she hangs over the side of her chair as if to say "look what I've done"!!

After such a fantastic month nine with Rosie getting to grips with everything, this month she got a viral infection. When babies get ill they lose their

appetites really quickly and it can take them some time before they get it back. Having been so used to her eating everything and anything, it has been hard to see her reject the things she would normally enjoy.

Having a weakness in the lungs (inherited from my side of the family), Rosie has been very wheezy with a nasty cough and this coming at a time when she had finally begun to sleep through the night. She sounds as if she smokes 20 a day and her sleep has been extremely disturbed. I have really struggled with both the lack of sleep and the number of breastfeeds she's wanted. If your baby gets ill, you may notice that they tend to eat lots of fruit and increase their need for milk feeds. They may also drop a little weight as it can take them a few weeks to recover their appetite after being ill. This is all perfectly normal so try not to worry.

Since being ill, Rosie's milk feeds have increased to around four a day. Sometimes she wakes early, so I give her a feed then (say around 5am) and again mid-morning, mid-afternoon and at bedtime. However, as her food intake starts to increase again I've no doubt that the milk feed will drop back to three a day or even less as she approaches 11 months old.

Having recovered from her illness, Rosie's favourite foods are fruit, (preferably cold from the fridge), yoghurt, porridge and flavoured rice cakes, all of which are particularly easy for her to manage.

It is so great that Rosie has her pincer grip as there really is no limit to what she can manage to eat. As soon as she is fully recovered I expect her to get seriously stuck into food again! She still has six teeth so no further progress there yet.

Chapter Nine

11 Months Old

If you haven't already done so, give your baby a spoon and a fork with their food and see how they get on. They will probably prefer the spoon for the time being but some will take to using a fork straight away. Some will have been capable of using the spoon for some time now and others may also be able to use the fork. However, in my experience they will still prefer to use their hands to feed themselves.

Worried parents often ask "when will my baby learn to eat properly?" The honest answer is that using a full set of cutlery is going to take some time. My little boy, who is coming up to four years old as I write this, still prefers using his hands to eat, especially when he is tired.

This doesn't mean that you shouldn't encourage them to use cutlery. In fact now is a good time to start setting a place for them at the family table. The idea is to start thinking about moving your baby from using the tray on the high chair, to eating at the main table. If you are using an Ikea highchair or similar, you can simply remove the tray and sit your baby directly at the table. By laying a place for them with cutlery, they can see themselves being incorporated into the family dining environment.

Most babies will have dropped their milk feeds down to a morning and evening feed by now. Although don't worry if your baby is still taking more than this. The guideline for formula-fed babies is three feeds a day/or 600ml. All babies are different, so do be guided by your baby. If they are eating really well and getting the calories and nutrients they need from food then their requirement for formula milk will be reduced.

Breastfed babies have been in control since day one! Since you don't know how much milk your baby is taking during a breast feed you are entirely guided by what they need. Rosie was eating so well by now that just one feed in the morning and one before bedtime lasting no more than 3 minutes each was enough to satisfy her needs.

Getting Ready for Baby's First Birthday

A baby's first birthday is a massive milestone and I'm sure you will want to celebrate in style. Once your baby turns 1 year old it will seem as if they suddenly go from being a baby to a little person.

When it comes to their first birthday you and those around you will want to treat your baby. Food is commonly used as a treat. However, without trying to spoil the party, remember that your baby does not know the difference between food for survival and food as a treat. Once again I recommend you hold off using food as a treat for as long as possible, including their first birthday – especially with regards to sweets and chocolate.

This does not stop you putting on a spread and allowing everyone to celebrate such an important event. You just need to follow the same principles you have been adhering to so far.

When you have a baby you tend to make friends with people who have babies of the same age, particularly if you are attending NCT classes or going to baby groups. All will be celebrating birthdays. This means that your child is going to have access to all sorts of foods that you may not want them to eat. From Haribo sweets to chocolate fingers to sausage rolls and finally to the iced and coloured cake, not to mention the party bags filled with goodness knows what!

It is still incredibly important (especially until they are five years old) to keep a check on your child's sugar and salt intake. And while you can have a healthy diet and still eat cake, there does need to be some control, especially where children are concerned.

Here are my suggestions for a first birthday party:-

To eat:-

- Finger sandwiches with wholemeal bread
  or mini pittas with hummus and grated carrot
- Cherry tomatoes

- Cucumber sticks
- Sweet Pepper strips (or use the baby ones quartered)
- Whole wheat bread sticks
- Homemade flapjacks (see recipe)
- Organix Tomato Noughts and Crosses crisps (or similar)
- Dried apricots
- Cheese sticks
- Flavoured rice cakes
- Grapes, blueberries and strawberries

This selection gives a huge variety of colour and children love colour.

If you have the time and energy you can also make:-

- Pitta bread pizza (just top a wholemeal pitta bread with a variety of toppings and bake in the oven)
- Homemade mini burgers
- Jacket potatoes
- Pasta salads
- Dips

For a cake I recommend a Chocolate Beetroot Cake (see recipe). This is a healthy recipe and the cake is topped with cream cheese.

For party bags:-

- A mini box of raisins
- A ginger bread man (homemade or use the Organix ones)
- A Satsuma
- A toy

If you can lead by example perhaps the other parents will follow suit!

Key Points

- Start thinking about moving your baby away from the highchair tray and make a place for them at the family dining table.
- If you haven't yet experimented with 'liquid' foods, now is a good time to try. Your baby may prefer to try meals like soup or stews from a small bowl or cup which they can tip and drink from.
- Try giving your baby a fork to use; some may well be able to 'stab' their food, although it is still a little early for most babies.

Rosie's Diary – Only Two Breastfeeds

11 Months Old

Rosie has recovered from her illness and as expected is back to normal eating and sleeping through the night. Hurray! She has now dropped her breastfeeds to one in the morning and one at bedtime. Very occasionally she may wake around 4am for an additional feed but this has probably only happened two or three times during the month. I still haven't had the opportunity to weigh her properly, although on our scales she is just over 1 ½ stone. Most of her clothes are size 9-12 months and are starting to look a little small.

Last week she cut a couple more teeth so she has six at the top, not in a row, and two at the bottom. Both of my children seem to cut their teeth at the same time as having a cold and cough, so as you can imagine it's been fun and games at our house.

If your baby has teeth please make sure that you get into the habit of cleaning them. We use an excellent product that Rosie can use by herself. It's called the Brush Baby Teether and is sold in John Lewis and Waitrose (you can also buy these from Amazon).

As you know all babies develop differently and it can be frustrating when everyone else's baby is doing things that yours can't do. Rosie has been static for quite some time. She is perfectly happy just sitting and observing everything and everyone around her. On the other hand her brother was crawling at eight months but didn't decide to walk until he was 16 months old. Rosie is currently showing no signs of wanting to crawl or pull herself up. She does, however, like to roll over and much prefers to sleep on her front. I expect that when she does finally crawl it won't be long before she gets up and walks. If you have more than one child then you will know why I am perfectly happy for her to be immobile for as long as she likes!

Meanwhile, eating out with a Baby-Led Weaning baby is so easy! We went to the Paralympics this month and decided to stop at Bluewater on the way back to have a meal at Wagamama. Both children thoroughly enjoyed their food and Rosie, as always, attracted plenty of attention because of her excellent eating skills for one so young. By now the two of them are used to eating all sorts of foods from different cultures and spicy foods are no different.

Rosie at home eating off a plate and enjoying her meal at Wagamama's Restaurant.

When your baby gets to this age (11 months) they will be eating so well and with such ease, that you often forget how young they actually are. Those on the puréed food route will be desperately trying to get some lumps into their food, but those on the Baby-Led Weaning route will be eating anything and everything (usually with their hands or with a spoon).

Something to watch out for at this stage is complacency. Make sure you have plenty of variety in your meals and once again make sure you are not letting salty or processed foods creep into their diet. Also keep an eye on those doting grandparents and their treats.

Try not to stick to the foods that you know your baby will eat, keep trying new recipes and foods to keep both you and your baby interested. Fussy eating starts to creep in when parents only give their children their favourite foods in order to have an easy life. Believe me, in the long run this leads to an extremely difficult life!! We have all met or know of children who will only eat fish fingers or pizza!!

Chapter Ten

One Year Old - What Happens Next

I bet you can't believe how quickly the months have passed. Give yourself a huge pat on the back because the journey you started six months ago has given your one-year-old child the best possible relationship they can have with healthy, home-cooked food. By giving your baby the same food as you eat and by including them in your family's normal eating routine, you have helped develop their coordination and motor skills as well as their social skills to the very best of their ability.

With regard to their milk intake there are a few options for you to consider:

If you are still breastfeeding, continue until you or your baby decides to stop. My children were 13 months and 15 months when they dropped milk feeds entirely. My little boy, who is dairy intolerant, took to drinking a cup of calcium fortified Rice Milk at bedtime. A cup a day of either Rice Milk or Soya Milk is fine for your baby, but both should be used in moderation as too much Soya Milk, which has oestrogenic properties, can affect their hormone balance; and Rice Milk contains traces of arsenic! However, there is no need to avoid them, as in the correct quantities they contain some valuable nutrients. Oat Milk and Unsweetened Almond Milk are also good substitutes for Cow's Milk. I tend to use either Almond milk or Soya milk at breakfast and Rice Milk in my cooking as it gives a nice sweet taste.

If you are starting to give your baby Cow's Milk, remember that your baby still needs a higher proportion of fat for their body weight compared to an adult, so don't change to semi-skimmed milk or low-fat dairy products until your baby is at least three years old.

Cow's Milk is often marketed as 'essential' milk for toddlers because of its calcium content, but if your baby doesn't want to drink Cow's Milk or will only drink a small amount, there's no need to worry as calcium is present in excellent quantities in many foods including almonds, broccoli, green leafy vegetables and sesame seeds. And because your baby is eating a varied and balanced diet, you can be confident that they are getting all the nutrients they need. When Rosie stopped breastfeeding she showed no interest in drinking any type of milk.

If you are using formula milk, then you may want to move on to Toddler Growing-Up Milk. It is worth noting, however, that whilst these formulas are sold as necessary to ensure your baby gets all the right nutrients, they are actually not necessary. To put this into perspective, a well-known formula milk brand claims that a toddler would need to drink an enormous beakerful of cow's milk to obtain the required daily intake of iron which is ridiculous as babies don't get their iron from milk! So all the advertisement does is put the worrisome idea into your head that your baby isn't getting enough iron, which simply isn't true if your baby is eating a balanced diet. Of course if you do want to use growing-up milk, there is nothing wrong with doing so.

If your baby is still being fed from a teated bottle, you can now move them on to a beaker. However, as most babies will find comfort in sucking on a teat, especially at bedtime, try giving them their milk in a beaker during the day. Your baby will probably have been using a beaker for water at mealtimes anyway so it shouldn't be difficult for them. Getting rid of the night-time bottle will probably take longer but don't worry too much about rushing this transition.

At this age, your baby will be extremely good at handling all sorts of food. However, liquid foods such as soup and stews may still present a challenge for a little while yet but don't let this put you off serving them. Give them to your baby in a small bowl or cup, perhaps with a little bread to help them soak up some of the liquid if they want to.

Going forward, simply continue giving them healthy food making sure you keep salt and sugar consumption low. Children aged one to three can only handle 2g of salt per day – less than a teaspoon.

You can give your baby honey now, as after their first birthday the risk of botulism is no longer a threat. But do remember that honey is still a sugar so don't go too mad!

Remember that the longer you can keep sweets and other sugary foods at bay, the better it is for your child. You may see these foods as a treat but to your child they are just something else to eat.

My little boy was just over three years old when we went to the Paralympics and bought some 'Olympic Special Edition Jellies'. He tasted sweets for the first time and thoroughly enjoyed them. Did this open the flood gates? No! The next time he had sweets was over 3 months later at Christmas. He is now coming up to four years old and never pesters us for sweets. He never even notices them when we are out shopping. It's not that we are depriving him of something, they simply don't feature in our daily lives. And the same is true for chocolate, biscuits and cakes (with the exception of the homemade ones we make together).

When I teach Baby-Led Weaning, I find that the entire family benefits from the positive changes in their diet. Keeping salt and sugar low and increasing your intake of foods such as whole grains, fruits and vegetables are key to keeping healthy and protecting the body against the onset of major diseases.

When you consider that one in four children starting primary school is already overweight, the effect of allowing a baby to self-feed cannot be overestimated. As a Mum and Nutritionist this makes me feel very positive about the future health of the next generation of children who have been weaned the baby-led way.

Continue to give your child access to good, healthy, home-cooked food and you truly will be doing the very, very best for them.

Key Points

- Lead by example and give your baby a healthy birthday by following the guide in this chapter.
- Continue to let your baby enjoy lots of different foods and dining experiences.
- Do keep having fun at mealtimes.

Rosie's Diary – First Birthday

1 Year Old

How quickly the time has flown. My baby is already one year old. She is such an accomplished feeder, eating many types of food and thoroughly enjoying every meal time. It is very easy to forget how young she still is.

For her birthday we had a family tea party with lots of presents, games and healthy foods, including her first ever no sugar chocolate cake, which she thoroughly enjoyed, even though it contained beetroot!

She has started to pull herself up a lot more and has been practising some bottom in the air manoeuvres in preparation for crawling. Her coordination is extremely well developed and she is very good at managing a spoon and a fork, although in typical Baby-Led Weaning style she prefers to use her hands. She particularly likes using her pincer grip and continues to delight in picking out any small foods such as peas or raisins, as if to say clever me. We had great fun with pomegranate seeds and I managed to catch that on video.

Rosie enjoying her presents and birthday cake (no sugar chocolate beetroot cake – see recipe)

Another food we tried for the first time this month was jelly. The texture and feel of the jelly really amuses young children and it's hilarious watching them play with it. Another item that is great fun for them to work with is a mango stone. You can only get so far slicing a mango and there is always some fruit left on the stone which makes a great game for any young child. The stone is really slippery and since the majority of babies LOVE mango, their determination to grab the stone, licking and gnawing the remains is a sight to behold!

By the time this one year milestone comes round your baby really will have mastered feeding themselves and Rosie is no different. The journey from here on will continue with her love of eating with the family and in the months to come learning more about food - growing it, preparing it, cooking it and eating the end result.

Chapter Eleven

Picky and Fussy Eaters

Around 18 months (although it could be earlier or later) nearly all children go through a phase of using food as a way to control their parents.

From your child's perspective they have very little control over anything in their lives and yet they are learning to become independent. It is an incredibly frustrating time for them.

Your child knows that they can probably incite a reaction from you around food and use it to their advantage!

It does seem that using Baby-Led Weaning reduces and limits the 'fussy' stage. This is probably because your baby has had complete control over their eating habits from day one and is used to eating all kinds of foods, textures and tastes.

The parents who have used the more traditional route of weaning (using purées and spoon feeding) have to go through the stage of introducing lumps and finger foods and the timing of this often coincides with this 'fussy' stage.

Another thing to consider is that your baby's growth rate starts to slow down at around 18 months. You only have to look at clothing sizes to see the difference compared to their growth rate from birth to twelve months old.

As your baby gets older the quantity of food they need reduces. Think back to the clothing size example. Your baby is growing rapidly in the first 12 months. After this their growth starts to slow down, so it makes sense that the amount of food they want and need is less.

The common mistake is to think that as your child gets bigger so should the size of the meal you give them. However, a large plateful of food can be overwhelming for a young child. Remember that their stomach is only the size of their two fists together. Keep the serving size small and if they eat it all, you can always give them some more. As soon as they are old enough, you can put the food on the table and get them to serve themselves. This way you can see exactly how much food they select.

Parents often make several mistakes when their child hits the fussy stage.

Firstly and understandably they get worried when their child starts leaving the food they would normally eat. The child senses this and realises very quickly that they can push your buttons. It is natural to be concerned when a child who has previously eaten really well starts to become picky and refuses meals. Refusing the odd meal or leaving certain foods is common so try not to worry. If your baby leaves an entire meal they are most likely not hungry.

Since you have weaned your baby using the Baby-Led Weaning method, you will be used to changes in their appetite from one day to another. Just like you, your baby will have days when they are really hungry and days when they want very little. So when the fussy stage starts, if you don't rise to the bait this phase will pass much quicker. However, with some children it can go on for quite a few months.

When your child starts leaving or refusing food your reaction may well be to give them something they particularly like instead. If you do this you are indicating that they can have whatever they like by refusing to eat what the rest of the family is eating. This is when fussy eating can become a real problem. You will no doubt have seen or heard about children who only eat chocolate biscuits or sausages – a direct result of parents offering foods they know the child really, really likes. This approach can get totally out of hand and before you know it you have a three year old who will only eat pizza!

Having a child go through this fussy stage is very stressful and can lead to anxiety at mealtimes. Your child will pick up on your tension which makes matters worse. You have to keep your cool. This is easier said than done but it will make a huge difference.

Never use food as a reward as it causes issues in the future. Never say things like "if you eat your vegetables you can have a sweet" because then you are signalling that vegetables aren't nice and sweets are. You also don't want your child to see certain food as a reward for being good in some way. "If you are a good boy or girl and let Mummy do her jobs, you can have a chocolate biscuit." You are setting them up to self-reward with food when they are older. You might even do this yourself when you've had a 'good' day or you've had some good news, thinking you'll treat yourself to a piece of cake! Special occasions are of course different, it's the day to day "if I'm good I can have" scenario which isn't healthy in the long run. While food is an essential part of life and should be enjoyed, eating needs to be a normal, stress-free daily activity.

So when your child starts to leave certain foods, simply accept it and keep on serving your usual family meals. They will eventually start eating them again.

Around this age your child will start developing their own tastes, so you need to recognise if the food they are avoiding is a food they really don't like, or if it's just the fussy phase they are going through. You might have noticed that your baby has suddenly stopped eating tomatoes which have been a favourite food up until now. This is part of the fussy phase. If on the other hand they have always picked at tomatoes, never going for them that much and then they suddenly stop eating them, the chances are that they have concluded that they simply don't like tomatoes.

You simply need to ride this phase out. Keep giving your child the same foods as the rest of the family and keep eating together as much as possible so that you can lead by example. Leading by example is extremely important. Keep the portions small and don't react if they leave their food.

Remember not to use food as a reward as they will quickly learn how to use this to their advantage. Never give an alternative, as this is where fussy eating can really become an issue. And make sure they are not filling up on snacks or drinks. Your child needs to be hungry to eat a meal otherwise they will quite naturally leave it.

If you are introducing new foods it can take a child up to twenty attempts before they decide if they like it.

Be aware that most children will tell you the food is disgusting or play up at mealtimes. If you continue to ignore these responses and give them the healthy foods that they have been eating previously, you will get over this phase without too much difficulty.

A child at this age won't starve themselves. If they are hungry they will eat the food you provide. It's your job to provide your child with food that is good for them. If you always do this then they won't know anything different.

It's also a good idea to get your child involved in food from a young age by reading books about food (such as the Hungry Caterpillar); play shops and games with plastic food; plant seeds and grow food in pots or in the garden; and make food together. Children love these activities and it really helps promote their healthy relationship with food.

Chapter Twelve

My Top Ten Foods for Young Children

These foods have been chosen specifically for their nutrient levels. Incorporating them into your child's diet on a regular basis will ensure that they receive an abundance of health promoting vitamins, minerals and essential fats.

Sweet potato

Bake, chip, mash, roast, and use in soups.

Children love this food with its orange flesh and lovely sweet skin.

- High in vitamin A (beta-carotene) and C, making it a great food for eye health.
- High in fibre, which helps the digestive system.
- Packed with antioxidants, which offers protection against many diseases.
- Contains a good range of B vitamins, which are essential for growth and development.
- A slow sugar release food which means you avoid peaks in blood sugar levels and maintain your energy for longer (a low glycaemic index food).

Avocado

Mashed avocado on toast is a great snack.

- A high protein fruit containing all essential amino acids needed for growth and repair.
- High in essential fats and vitamin E which help keep blood thin, cholesterol low and the brain and heart healthy.
- Eaten with other foods it aids digestion.
- Contains vitamin K to make sure bones grow properly.

Kiwi

Simply quarter this fruit with the skin left on and let them eat the insides.

When using kiwi in a smoothie leave the skin on as it is full of nutrients and they will not notice the difference. You can make a thick smoothie for your baby to eat with a spoon or give them a small (open topped) cup to try and drink from.

- Contains more vitamin C than oranges, which is vital for the immune system and for helping the absorption of iron.

Dried Apricots

Use as a snack, add to meat dishes - lamb with apricots is really delicious, also great in cakes and biscuits.

- A good source of iron and potassium.
- High in beta-carotene essential for growth, immunity and eye health.

Buy the unsulphured variety if your child is asthmatic, as this additive can be a trigger.

Quinoa

Use as a healthy alternative to potato, rice, pasta and couscous. Try it cooked in orange juice with raisins.

Most supermarkets now stock this product, which is an ancient grain and has been around for thousands of years.

- Contains all nine essential amino acids, important for growth and repair.
- Contains calcium, magnesium, potassium and B3.
- Is a gluten free grain and extremely good for the digestive system.

Almonds

You can use these ground for children under three and add it to their porridge or breakfast cereal or use as a nut butter. You can buy nut butters in health food shops or simply blend the nuts until they are a spreadable consistency and put them on rice cakes, bread or crackers. I use ground almonds in some of my dinner recipes. I also use almond milk.

- Contains essential fats which help keep the cardiovascular system healthy.
- A good source of calcium needed for strong and healthy bones.
- High in vitamin E which helps to keep the blood thin.
- A nutrient rich food including vitamins and the minerals magnesium and potassium.

Hummus

Homemade hummus is a fantastic food for children. You can use it in so many ways: instead of mayonnaise; as a sandwich filling with grated carrot; as a jacket potato filling; or simply add a dollop to chilli and rice.

Mash chickpeas, olive oil, tahini (ground sesame seeds), garlic, lemon juice and paprika together, or whizz in a blender for a smoother consistency.

You can buy it ready-made, although the nutrient content will be much less and remember to check the salt content.

- High in fibre.
- Good source of protein.
- Full of essential fats, vitamins and minerals including calcium.

Salmon (or any oily fish)

In the early days of weaning if you steam salmon and mix it with some mashed potato you can easily load it onto a spoon for your baby to eat.

Make into fish fingers, fishcakes, and use left-over salmon mixed with a little hummus to make a delicious sandwich filling.

- Contains omega 3 fats which are essential for the brain, heart and immune system.
- Omega 3 also acts as an anti-inflammatory - important for conditions like eczema and asthma.

It is important to note that the body cannot make Omega 3 fats, so they must come from food. Omega 3 is also found in mackerel, tuna, herring, trout and sardines.

Oats

Make porridge. Also soft flapjacks (see recipe).

- High in fibre.
- Contain a good supply of vitamins, minerals and phyto-nutrients.
- Contains Beta glucans which are important for keeping bad cholesterol levels down.
- Oats release their sugar slowly avoiding peaks in blood sugar levels and maintaining energy for longer.

Spinach

Until your child has some teeth, green leafy foods can be difficult for them to eat. One of the best ways to include them in their diet is in a smoothie or home-made lolly. Simply add a handful to any blended fruits and they will never know it is there.

- Contains the minerals iron, magnesium and calcium.
- Contains the vitamins folic acid, B-vitamins and vitamin C.

Chapter Thirteen

What the Parents Have to Say

There is nothing quite like hearing from the horse's mouth, so I have included some pictures and comments from parents who would like to urge you to practise Baby-Led Weaning.

"Even though my twin boys were born 6 weeks early, I still started weaning at 6 months and they took to self-feeding like it was second nature. Watching them discover food for themselves at such a young age was amazing. I would not hesitate to recommend Baby-Led Weaning to new parents, especially parents of multiples." *Nicola, Mum to Twins Alex and William*

"As our eldest child Martha approached 6 months our attention turned to weaning! Baby-Led Weaning immediately appealed as Martha had been exclusively breastfed to that point and it seemed to follow on nicely in that she was already competent at letting us know when she was hungry and determining her own portion sizes! Having said that, we didn't know anyone else who had weaned their child in this way and anyone we mentioned it to seemed to look at us in complete horror!

In the end we started making and puréeing her food but we were quickly disheartened as it was time consuming and she wasn't really that interested! Thankfully when Martha was around 8 months I heard about Julie's Baby-Led Weaning course and eagerly signed up. It was great to learn more about Baby-Led Weaning and I quickly gained confidence in this method after talking to the other parents. We didn't look back, we stopped puréeing and Martha's interest in food quickly picked up. She enjoyed sampling and working out how best to eat whatever we offered. A couple of months later we were invited to a family dinner - Martha loved every minute, joining in this sociable exchange as much as any of the adults. Sitting at the head of the table she became the focal point and an hour later was completely covered in food but happy and full up! With Martha competently feeding herself we were able to eat and enjoy our meal too. By her first birthday she could point out diverse fruits and vegetables whilst on our weekly shopping trip and being an early and clear talker she could name them all soon after!

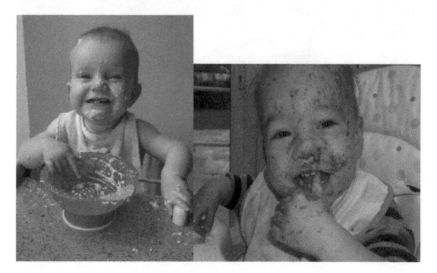

Our son William, who was born a couple of years later, was completely Baby self-fed and we have never spoon fed him a single meal. The first few months especially can be a messy business but food becomes fun instead of a chore! We had what we called 'eating clothes' which consisted of a couple of pairs of old jogging bottoms and t-shirts, which we pulled on whenever it was time for a meal. Will amazed friends and family with his eating skills, he could drink from a cup without a lid at the age of 10 months and use a spoon to feed himself competently soon after his first birthday! Our working hours meant that we got to eat dinner together every night which is lovely as the children quickly learnt table manners and important social skills and Will obviously copies his elder sister as well as us.

Baby-Led Weaning makes this stage of growing up fun and we hope Martha and Will have developed a healthy approach to food and eating which will last a lifetime!" *Claire, Mum to Martha and William*

"Annabel was 8 months old when we took her to visit my mother-in-law in France. As you can see we went out for lunch, where Annabel ploughed her way through a sausage, baked potato, corn on the cob, green beans and anything else we gave her. She sat in her high chair for two hours happily chatting and eating - my Mother-in-law was gobsmacked and said that none of her four children would do that until they were at least 2yrs!" *Vanessa, Mum to Annabel*

"This is my son Samuel eating apple and bypassing scrambled eggs at age eight months. Apple has been one of his staple favourites almost since the beginning of weaning. He still hasn't eaten scrambled eggs to this day!" *Cheryl, Mum to Samuel*

"This is my son Louis aged 9 months tucking into 'Spag-a-sausage'. Louis has silent reflux and didn't take to traditional weaning. We had a very stressful few weeks trying to feed him purées whilst his dietician was insisting I needed to give him less breast milk and feed him proper food. We took this advice with a pinch of salt. However, I can happily say that we now offer Louis a bit of what we're having and he tries everything. His favourite foods are hummus, cherry tomatoes and strawberries! No purées and he can have breast milk whenever he likes. We love Baby-Led Weaning in our house." *Melanie, Mum to Louis*

"Baby-Led Weaning was without doubt one of the best parenting decisions that we have made since Harry was born. Harry took to it really well and although he gagged quite a lot for the first 2 weeks, it was much worse for us than it was for him. Within a week he was managing to use a spoon for his yoghurt. My husband and I were, and continue to be, amazed at not only how easy Baby-Led Weaning was for us but also how much fun it was for Harry. We loved watching him discover new food tastes and textures and still marvel today (he's now 17 months) at how well he eats. I attended Julie's Baby-Led Weaning course which I have found invaluable, particularly for the nutritional advice that she gave. Harry is definitely eating a wider variety of foods and much healthier foods because I had the basics to follow and some easy recipes to make. In fact we are all eating much more healthily as a result of the course. I am now expecting baby number 2 and will definitely be doing BLW again when the time comes." *Jo, Mum to Harry*

"Maria aged 9 months showing how much fun it is to eat Spaghetti Bolognese" *Laura, Mum to Maria*

"Izzy, enjoying her corn on the cob" *Amy, Mum to Izzy*

"Madi shows how well equipped she is at managing a variety foods at just six months old!" *Charlotte, Mum to Madi*

"I had never heard of Baby-Led Weaning when we first started solids at 5½ months, but Eva refused purées right from the start. I gave her a whole banana and never looked back. Some of her favourites are tomatoes, broccoli and asparagus. It was a little scary at first when she gagged, but she learned really fast and by 8 months she was a pro!" *Eva and Dad Riley*

"I believe that Baby-Led Weaning is the only way to introduce food to your child from 6 months of age. I have successfully weaned both my children this way having attended Julie's course and I have encouraged others to do the same. Their Grandparents were astounded at how quickly they were able to join in eating Sunday lunch.

My eldest son took to it like a duck to water and continues to enjoy a variety of foods, and although my youngest son was more tentative at first, he is now on track and as you can see from the photo he is enjoying a homemade lasagne and using it to colour his face and hair! Make sure you save bolognese and lasagne for just before bath time!" *Diane, Mum to Noah*

"It was slow going at first and Dexter didn't really swallow for the first 4-6 weeks. He would try any food I put in front of him though! Then all of a sudden about 8 weeks in (when he'd just turned 8 months) it 'clicked'. Since then we've gone from strength to strength." *Vicky, Mum to Dexter*

"The Happy Little Eaters course changed our family eating for the better. Baby-Led Weaning my two babies gave me confidence that our job, as parents, is to offer a selection of healthy food and set a good example. I have always been able to take my two girls out for lunch, with all of us enjoying the food and company. I highly recommend a whole family approach to weaning - as children are the best imitators."
Lydia, Mum to Gladys

"Baby-Led Weaning is one of the best choices I made for my son. Jesse is not fussy at all and eats lots of healthy foods."
Sophie, Mum to Jesse

"This is one if the many pictures I have of Henry demonstrating Baby-Led Weaning. In this one he nicked a whole apricot off the window ledge and just tucked in!" *Jemma, Mum to Henry*

Chapter Fourteen

My Family Favourite Recipes

These recipes have been tried and tested on my children throughout their Baby-Led Weaning journey. Whilst there are a number of excellent cookery books on the subject of Baby-Led Weaning, you can adapt almost any family recipe in to a baby friendly version.

Note

Xylitol (marketed under the brand name Total Sweet) is a natural sugar alternative and I have used this in many of my 'sweet' recipes to make them more healthy. Xylitol comes from the birch tree and has a low GI (glycaemic index value) meaning it does not raise blood sugar levels when consumed, making it also safe for diabetics. Evidence has also shown it to protect against tooth decay. However, intake should be restricted and only used for treat purposes as excessive use can cause digestive discomfort.

Tip

Mash any beans or pulses until your baby has mastered their pincer grip.

Snack Recipes

Soft Almond & Apricot Flapjacks

- 250g raisins
- 50g dried apricots
- 75ml olive oil
- 250g porridge oats
- 50g ground almonds

1. Set the oven to 180 degrees C/gas 4/350 degree Fahrenheit.
2. Place raisins and apricots in a small pan and just cover with water. Heat gently to soften.

3. Place contents of pan in a food processor/liquidiser and blitz. Transfer to a bowl.
4. Add the olive oil, oats and almonds and mix together.
5. Place mixture into a shallow cake tin (approx. 27x18cm) and press down. Mixture should be about 2-3cm thick.
6. Bake for 20-25 minutes until lightly browned on top. Allow to cool in the tin.

Carrot, Orange and Raisin Muffins – Makes about 10

- 150g of self-raising flour (you can also use Dove's wheat free flour for this recipe)
- 60g butter (or you can use dairy free spread suitable for baking)
- 2 large eggs beaten
- 2 medium carrots grated
- Juice and zest of one large orange
- A handful of raisins

1. Preheat oven to 10C/373F/Gas 5
2. Add a muffin case to 10 sections of a muffin tin
3. Sieve flour into a large bowl
4. Melt the butter in a saucepan and in a separate bowl combine the eggs, carrot, raisins and orange and add the melted butter
5. Pour the mixture into the flour and fold in
6. Spoon about a tablespoon of mixture into each of the muffin cases
7. Bake for 10-15 minutes
8. Cool and enjoy

Chocolate Beetroot Cake with Cream Cheese Frosting - Serves 10

- 200g plain flour or gluten free plain flour
- ½ tsp bicarbonate of soda
- 1 tsp of baking powder (gluten free baking powders are available from health food shops)
- ½ tsp salt
- 100g Xylitol (branded Total Sweet in the supermarket)
- 2 medium size organic eggs
- 180ml olive oil

- 170g good quality dark chocolate
- 225g grated raw beetroot (or you could use courgette or butternut squash)

For the cream cheese frosting
- 250g low fat cream cheese
- ½ tsp vanilla extract
- 1 tbsp Xylitol

1. Preheat oven to 180C/350F/Gas 4. Line the base of a 20cm cake tin with baking paper and grease the sides.
2. Stir the flour, bicarb, baking powder and salt into a bowl and add the xylitol. Mix well.
3. In a separate bowl beat the eggs into the oil.
4. Melt the chocolate by placing in a bowl and then put into a saucepan of water. Do not let the water come in contact with the chocolate.
5. Stir the eggs and oil mix in to the dry mix and add the melted chocolate, beetroot and nuts (if using).
6. Pour the mixture into the cake tin and bake for 30 mins or until the cake is well risen and firm to touch, a skewer or wooden stick should come out clean.
7. Allow to cool before icing.
8. Mix together the cream cheese, vanilla and xylitol. Spread on to the cooled cake.

Dips and Spreads
Hummus

- 400g can of chickpeas, drained and rinsed
- juice of 1 lemon
- 3 tbsps of olive oil
- 1 tbsp of tahini (this is ground sesame seeds)
- 1 garlic clove, crushed
- black pepper and paprika to taste

1. Add all of the ingredients together in a blender and blend until smooth

Skordalia

- 300g celeriac root, peeled & cut into small cubes
- 125g potato, cubed
- 3 garlic cloves, crushed
- 100ml of milk (any type)
- 100ml of olive oil

1. Boil the potato and celeriac until tender (about 15mins). Drain until dry
2. In a blender, blend until smooth and then add the garlic and blend again
3. Warm the milk and add to the olive oil
4. Add the milk & oil slowly through the top of the blender whilst running
5. When the mixture is smooth and silky it's ready to serve

Dinner Recipes

Lentil Dhal – Serves 4 (can be frozen)

- 300g red lentils, well rinsed
- 600ml water
- 1 medium onion chopped
- 4 cloves garlic crushed
- 1 x 400g can of chopped tomatoes
- 1 tsp curry powder

1. Place the lentils, onion and garlic in a saucepan with the water. Bring to the boil and simmer for 10 minutes.
2. Add the remaining ingredients and stir well. Cover and simmer for 20 minutes (keep an eye on this as it can stick to the pan, add more water if needed).
3. Serve this with steamed vegetables and brown rice or quinoa.

Pea, Ham and Potato Omelette – Serves 4

- Approximately 3 small part boiled potatoes
- Olive oil for frying
- 1 onion, chopped

- 5-8 eggs (depending on size of your frying pan)
- A thick slice of ham, cubed or chorizo/pancetta
- Handful of frozen peas

1. Thickly slice the cooled potato and fry in a large pan with the olive oil and onion until softened.
2. Add the peas and ham and fry for a couple of minutes.
3. In a large bowl, beat the eggs and then add to the frying pan, covering all of the ingredients.
4. Preheat the grill to high.
5. Cook the omelette for about 10 minutes until half set, then place pan under grill and cook for a further 10 - 15 minutes until the omelette is golden.
6. Serve in wedges adding a side salad.

Vegetarian Chilli - Serves 4 (can be frozen)

- 1 small onion, peeled and finely chopped
- 1 clove garlic, peeled and crushed
- 1 tsp of olive oil
- 125g mushrooms, finely chopped
- 1 small aubergine, finely diced
- 1 tbsp tomato purée
- 400g tin of chopped tomatoes
- 100ml of vegetable stock
- ½ - 2 tsp chilli powder (depending how hot you like it)
- ½ tsp ground cumin
- a pinch of mixed herbs
- 400g tin of red kidney beans (drained)

1. Gently cook the onion and garlic in the olive oil until soft. Add the mushrooms, aubergines, tomato purée, chopped tomatoes, stock, spices and herbs and bring to the boil.
2. Reduce the heat and add the kidney beans, simmer for 30 minutes, stirring from time to time.
3. Serve with brown rice or taco shell and salad.

Moroccan Chickpea Stew – serves 4

- 400g can of chickpeas drained and rinsed
- 4 tbsp olive oil
- 2 red onions sliced
- 2 garlic cloves crushed
- 1 tsp ground turmeric
- 1 tsp ground ginger
- 1 tsp ground cumin
- ½ tsp ground cinnamon
- 400g can of chopped tomatoes
- 600ml vegetable stock (or use water)
- 200g cooked brown rice

1. Heat oil in a large pan and fry the garlic, spices and onion until soft.
2. Add tomatoes, chickpeas and stock. Cover and simmer for 20 minutes.
3. Stir in the cooked rice and serve (you can also add some fresh chopped coriander when you add the rice and/or fresh red chillies).

Butternut Squash Curry – Serves 4 (can be frozen)

- 1 tbsp of olive oil
- 2 red onions chopped
- 4 cloves of garlic crushed
- 1 medium butternut squash, peeled, deseeded and cubed
- 1 inch of fresh ginger grated
- 2 tsp of curry powder
- 60ml of vegetable stock (or use water for the babies)
- 300ml of coconut milk
- 100g red lentils (wash before use)
- 400g can tomatoes, chopped
- 4 tbsp baby leaf spinach
- Fresh coriander
- Black pepper

1. Heat the oil in a saucepan and sauté onion and garlic for 5 minutes to soften.
2. Stir in the butternut squash and curry powder, pour in the stock, lentils and tomatoes and bring to the boil.

3. Cover and simmer for 1 hour, stirring occasionally.
4. Stir in the spinach and allow to wilt.
5. Add the coriander and pepper.
6. Serve with brown rice.

Baked Falafel – Makes approx 12

- Wholemeal pittas
- 400g can chickpeas, well drained
- 1 red onion, roughly chopped
- 1/4 cup wholegrain spelt flour
- 3 tbsp fresh parsley
- 1-2 garlic cloves
- 1 tsp ground cumin
- 3/4 tsp salt (optional)
- 1/2 tsp baking powder
- 1/4 tsp lemon juice
- Sprinkle of paprika, or more to taste
- Black pepper, to taste
- Baby spinach (toppings – not to be included in the falafel mixture)
- Avocado chopped (toppings – not to be included in the falafel mixture)
- Diced tomatoes (toppings – not to be included in the falafel mixture)

1. Preheat oven to 180C. Place all ingredients for falafel (except for the pittas, spinach, tomatoes and avocado) in a food processor and whizz briefly so the mixture isn't too smooth.
2. Transfer into a bowl, add the baking powder and stir together.
3. Line a baking tray with baking paper. One at a time, take spoonfuls of mixture in your hands and form 15 balls, each about the size of a ping pong ball, and gently place them on the baking sheet.
4. Bake in the oven for 15 minutes (note – depending on your oven, this might take longer – up to 20-25 minutes – but be sure to check on them to make sure the bottom doesn't burn!).
5. Serve in a warm pitta with the spinach, avocado and tomatoes plus a dollop of hummus or on their own with some sweet potato wedges and salad.

Dessert Recipe
Homemade Lollies

You can buy lolly moulds from lots of places; try the supermarket, pound shop and Lakeland. The ones with the juice catcher at the bottom are brilliant for little ones.

A Simple Fruit Lolly – dilute some fresh juice (any flavour you like) with water using at least half and half and then freeze in lolly moulds.

Spinach Delight Lolly – in a blender add some pineapple, spinach leaves plus water to dilute and blitz. Freeze in the lolly moulds. Your child will never know there is spinach in their lolly!

Strawberry Smoothie Lolly – in a blender add strawberries, natural yoghurt and water to dilute and blitz.

Vegetable Lolly – in a juicer place enough carrots and apples plus a very little ginger to fill a tray of moulds. Dilute if needed and freeze.

You can try all sorts of varieties and it's great to experiment and see which ones your children like the best.

Lollies are also a great teether for sore gums.

Chapter Fifteen

The Final Word

I cannot emphasise enough the importance of providing nutrient dense, natural whole food, especially in the first five years while your children are developing their tastes and appetite control.

Until your child starts school you have complete control over what food they have access to and what, as a family, you choose to eat together. Even if your child goes to nursery you can still be quite specific about which foods and drinks you allow them to have and which you do not.

As I write this, my little boy is four years old and has completed his first full term at school. He is a very good eater and enjoys a wide range of different foods. His absolute favourite food is fruit, the more exotic the better. I make a packed lunch for him to take to school because I still want to be in charge of what he eats. He likes to get involved in the decision making process of what goes into his lunch bag and always opts for healthy foods, choosing crackers, carrot sticks, hummus, blueberries etc. He also enjoyed tuna sandwiches until someone called him tuna breath and now refuses to take them to school. He still eats them at home, but gets upset if I try to include them in his lunch bag.

He has started asking about crisps and 'squeezy' foods which the other children presumably have in their lunch boxes. You cannot underestimate the influence other children have on your child but if you provide and continue to provide good healthy food at home, you know that they are getting a well rounded diet.

By having set them off on their self-feeding journey, you have helped them to develop their appetite control and refine their tastes. As an example, in my family, when I make homemade biscuits together with my children, we use wholegrain spelt flour, olive oil, cinnamon and a little agave syrup. My children love them. However, when other children visit our house to play, they tend to take one bite and leave the rest. My conclusion is that our biscuits are not sweet enough for their taste. This saddens me a little because sugar is a problem.

Sugar is making headline news with articles entitled *'Sweet, Dangerous and Deadly'*! Sugar has no nutritional value whatsoeverand is addictive. A recent study identified that sugar activates the part of the brain associated with drug and alcohol addiction. How scary is that!? Particularly when we know that it is added to almost all manufactured foods. And I truly believe that sugar is at the root of many of our most prevalent diseases.

Until fairly recently our main source of sugar came from starchy vegetables and fruits. These days it is possible to exceed our recommended daily intake of sugar by eating a so called 'healthy' breakfast with yoghurts and breakfast cereals being loaded with sugar. Almost all foods aimed at our youngsters are laced with sugar, ensuring that children will come back for more, filling the pockets of food manufacturing companies.

In his book *"Pure, White and Deadly"* John Yudkin identified that sugar consumption has risen dramatically in the last 200 years from less than 5 pounds per person per year, to a whopping 120 pounds per person per year. To put that in perspective, we now manage to eat a whole year's supply of sugar in 2 weeks! And the biggest consumers of sugar are teenage boys - great news if you are in the sugar business!

The example of our homemade biscuits gives me confidence that my own children don't have a sweet tooth, a result which you too can easily achieve with your own children.

Rosie, who is now 2 years old, continues to eat incredibly well. Her favourite foods are olives, apples, hummus and brown rice. She astounds people with the quantity of food she eats, as well as the types of food she selects.

I firmly believe that the way my children eat is not down to luck or chance. They simply do not know any different. We, as parents, lead by example and so have the opportunity to give our children access to good wholesome and nutritious food. Of course, this doesn't mean we have to be saints or health freaks. We also like 'treats' but if we keep these to around 5 - 10% of our overall intake, the body can cope with that level, especially when combined with a nutrient rich diet.

Please read food labels so that you know what is in the food you are giving your children and yourself for that matter. If a product contains sugar within the first three ingredients, it is not a good choice. If it contains over 10g per 100g know that that is a lot of sugar. If a label contains ingredients you can't pronounce, it can't be good for you! The best foods come without a label!

Here, Rosie is enjoying a homemade berry lolly and Charlie has melon.

The Author

"I believe passionately in the education and promotion of good nutrition to empower the general public to take responsibility for their health and well-being.

"When ill health led me to seek help from a nutritionist, the results were so dramatic that it became my vocation. Since qualifying I have been running a busy clinic in the south east of England offering one-to-one consultations, as well as running group sessions, courses and giving talks.

"After the birth of my first child in 2009, my health visitor recommended a whole-food approach to weaning babies. The information was so in tune with my own work that I weaned both first and second child in this way. Feeling passionately about giving babies the best start in life, I've added healthy eating for babies to my skill-set and run weekly parent and baby groups called *Happy Little Eaters*, which gives new parents valuable advice on weaning, baby nutrition and healthy diets for all the family."

Julie Clark

Spring Nutrition was set up by Julie to offer clients the advice and help they need to lead a long and healthy life.

- One to One consultations (adults and children)
- Family Consultation
- Baby-Led Weaning Course
- Fussy Eater Help
- Yummy Mummy Online Course

www.spring-nutrition.co.uk

Find us on Facebook **'Spring Nutrition'** and Twitter **@springnutri**